Big & Little
DogSpirations

We Love Them—They Inspire Us

Big & Little

DogSpirations

We Love Them—They Inspire Us

Dee Aspin

www.DeeAspin.com
deeaspin@deeaspin.com

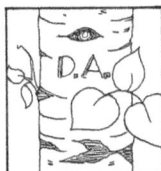

BARK LEAF PRESS

BARKLEAF PRESS
Sacramento, CA

Big and Little Dogspirations:
We Love Them—They Inspire Us

COPYRIGHT 2022 by Dee Aspin
First edition published as dogSpirations, 2015

ISBN_13: 978-0-9829093-5-5
Library of Congress Control Number: 2021924141

BarkLeaf Press
Sacramento, CA

Graphic cover by ©Steve Powell
Dogs at Wedding, 2012 ©Kathy Boyd-Fellure,
http://www.kathyboydfellure.com/
Doggie Heaven illustration, 2021 ©E.V. Sparrow
http://sparrow.world
Dogs in Studio, 2012 ©Gary Gauthier
All other photos in book ©Dee Aspin
PawPrint graphics, 2015 ©Julie Williams

Printed in United States of America

These stories are based on actual incidences. They may sound like someone you know who has similar situations. Confidentiality has been observed in certain cases and names or minor circumstances have been changed.

Dedicated to Samson Paul
My Glimpse of Heaven

When I look into your steadfast eyes,
I see the clearest bluest skies;
No brokenness from hammered earth,
Raised in our home from puppy-birth.
And God has covered my mistakes
When I've felt regretful aches,
From times I acted immature,
Because I handled anger poor.
But always loving,
You've forgiven…
You are my closest glimpse of heaven.

Your patience and faithful love to me will always
be a glimmer of the divine nature of our Creator.

Special Thanks

Inspire Writers Group

Thank you for your support and help crafting these devotions over the past seven years.

Elizabeth Thompson, Beth Cantrell, Dana Sudboro, John Kaschak, Chris Pedersen, Kris Lindsey, Kathy Boyd Fellure, Lori Sinclair, Michelle Hamilton, Joanne Kraft, Jennifer Hamilton, Cheri Douglas, Elaine Faber, Sheila Alford, Sandra Trezise Heaton, Scotti Fritts, Maureen Noumov, Ellen Cardwell, Sherri Bergmann, Chris Drzewiecki, Linda Sellers, Erin Bamberry, Diane Dolan, Lenore Buth, Sue Geranen, Susan Wright & more!

Special thanks to E.V. Sparrow, Julie Williams, Katie Young, and Nancy Broadhurst.

My Famiglia

Who welcomed Sam and Benji, and now Lassen and Lily, as "Part of the Family."

For all your years of dog sitting and caring for all my dogs—Mom of "Nona's Doggie Daycare," Dad, "Grandpa," Uncle Mike and Tim, David, Patrick, Chris and Sean—my brothers and nephews, who loved them and wrestled with them. Their doggie cousins, Troy the braveheart. And Shasta, now in Doggie Heaven.

The girls in the family who love dogs—Nicole, Robin, Pamela, Lynette, Kristen, and Lauren.

Travis, Adam, and of course my hubby, our Alpha Dog—Steve!

And Friends

Who have cared for them—Gary, Donna, Robyn, Melinda, Erin, Erika, Pam, Karen, Dee, Victoria, Lanie, Nancy H, Pres, Janice Brown, Karen and Mark Roberts.

Contents

Dedicated to Samson Paul
My Glimpse of Heaven. vii

Special Thanks ix

Introduction. xv

    Welcoming Committee .1

    In the Master's Shadow. 5

    It's a Dog, Dog, Dog, Dog World 9

    I am Mickey, Not Maude 13

    Expand Your Territory. 15

    Triggers. 18

    Privilege 22

    Haircuts. 26

    Chocolate 29

    Dog on the Loose 34

    Bone Wars. 38

Mickey's Magic Meatball 41

Feed My Need. 44

Hills. 48

It's the Fight in the Dog 52

Blast from the Past 57

Dogs Teach 61

Five O'Clock and All is Well 62

Surrender. 65

Special. 69

Doggie Park Day. 73

Sammy's Dreams 76

Chasing the White Cat . . . . , . .79

The Dynamic Duo. 82

Lab without Borders 87

Instincts. 91

Observe, Observe, Observe. 95

Small Sticks 99

Me Too 104

Leashes 109

The Rooster and the Beast 113

There Are Other Dogs, Too. 118

Enchanting Ears 122

The Trouble with Coyotes. 126

Oasis around the Bend 130

That Thing You Do 134

No to the Nose 137

Hidden Treasures 141

Keeping Up with the Boneses. 145

Beyond the Blinds. 150

Doggie Seconds 154

Samson's Turning Tide 158

Seasons Change 163

Groans of Love 166

Indecision 170

Terms of Endearment 173

The Ball is in the Big Dog's Court 178

Leave It. 181

Reflections from the Zoo 185

Fascinations. 189

He's a Keeper 192

One Disenchanted Night. 196

Acceptance 200

Barriers 204

Rescue. 206

Doggie Heaven: *The following section includes five devotionals about the time our pets leave us*

Shelby's Crossover 214

It's Friday but Sunday's Coming. 217

Divine Interruptions .221

Happy Tails to You
Until We Meet Again 225

Doggie Heaven 235

Closing Thoughts: *Reflections of a dog owner*

Circle of Life. 238

Closing—Dog Family. 246

About the Author. 248

Also by Dee Aspin 249

Introduction

I never thought I needed a dog until I grew up. As a child, German Shepherds were part of our household—but not a part of my heart. I fed them when reminded and jogged with them in high school. In college I brought home strays—but they never stuck around.

Hannah, a black Lab/Rot mix, walked into my life one busy ER night shift, dumped off at the ambulance dock. So began my love for Labs. Mickey, a miniature-schnauzer I watched "temporarily" to help out my friend's homeless son, broke my obsession with big dogs. I learned to love the littles.

My journal entries included dog experiences that dovetailed with my Scripture readings. Pets exponentially enhanced my daily enjoyment of life. After Mickey died, I planned a dog family, chose two breeds and purchased puppies.

I adapted Sammy at seven weeks old, my yellow Lab puppy, followed by Pepper six months later and Benji three years later—two miniature schnauzers.

Soon more devotionals tumbled from my heart and mind like an open faucet. Moments with my dogs, my fur-babies, timed in a way God could get my attention, taught me lessons I needed to learn about myself, others, and God's character…experiences I felt compelled to share.

Most lessons were written as a single woman until God surprised me with a husband. Steve's grey beard matched Benji's—so, I affectionately nicknamed him, my giant schnauzer. Our wedding day overflowed with delight, enhanced by Benji and Sam in matching black ties. Sam joyfully and Benji, not-so-joyfully, accompanied two cute ring bearers down the aisle to our wedding processional—a special moment celebrating our love.

The joy our animals bring, the seasons of life they represent and store in our memory is an album of beautiful music that never fades. It lives on inside of us.

Dogs are an amazing gift from God.
Ever-present furry angels,
They are loving and demanding,
curious and understanding—
Dawn to dawn, dusk to dusk—
Except when they are sleeping,
Under our safe keeping…

I cannot imagine a life without love and humor, God and prayer, family and friends—and pets. For me it is dogs.

Dogs inspire little life lessons and big God glimpses…dogSpirations.

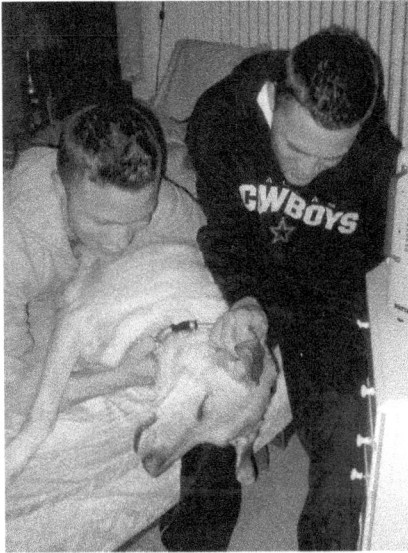

*My nephews, David and Patrick, enjoying
a good wrestle with Sammy the family dog.*

Welcoming Committee

Ding, dong. The doorbell sparked a blast of dog drama from the garage. *Woof, woof. Yeep, yeep.* I looked up from the computer and glimpsed Dad's gray jacket and black baseball cap through the branches outside my study window.

"Just a minute, Dad!" I yelled and veered around the corner to the hall garage entrance and opened the door. Two dog-o-motives rushed by, a little engine and a big caboose.

"Oohhh—what's that noise?" Dad's voice rose from the entrance over the barks. "Hee, hee! Hee hee!" His face crinkled like Santa Claus as he patted his welcoming committee. "No one greets me like you guys!"

Something resounded from lunch with a friend the week prior—she had described a conversation with her husband during their engagement. "Before we married, my husband gave up his dog, Capri. He thought someone else could give her more exclusive attention than he would be able to. 'Are you sure you want to do that?' I had asked him.

"Now he misses her." She frowned. "He misses coming home to a big fuss like he's the reason for everything."

She shook her head. "I warned him up front, 'I will never greet you like Capri does.'"

Dogs have an uncanny ability to make us feel special. I think that's why God created animals before man in His grand design for all creation. He put them in the garden to welcome Adam and Eve. They still help us feel at home—and teach us a few things, including how to bond and love.

A couple days ago, I knelt to put water in Sam's big water bowl. He appreciates fresh water. I need to fill his bowl sooner and not wait so long.

He ambled over and put his nose near mine. *Slurp.* He left a big damp kiss on my cheek. I looked at him and smiled. "Thanks Sam." His eyes gleamed into mine before he turned around and sauntered back to his spot on the garage floor.

He's not only my welcoming committee, but my gratitude bearer as well.

Sam's timing couldn't have been better. Because after filling his bowl it was time to gather the doggie bags and clean the side yard, his outhouse, for garbage day tomorrow. Maybe Sam knew I was tired. Maybe he heard my sighs. His little gesture of appreciation helped me muster the energy I needed for cleaning his dog pad—it's a major chore when my back is bothersome.

I think every dog owner relates to this weary work of maintenance through the changing seasons. Summer and winter doo-doo pickup becomes a well-worn path we all circle habitually day in, day out—especially with big dogs.

Then there's the inside clean-up that Benji brings with his bad habit of garbage intruder.

Last week I ventured to the 99-cent store to pick up childproof locks needed to keep Benji from getting into trouble when I'm gone. He discovered two weeks ago how to open the cupboard under the kitchen sink. Every day since then, the floor mat is strewn with paper towels and banana skins.

We bend and adjust to fit our dogs into our lives. We tend to the little messes and the big ones. Why? Because we are daily applauded just for being present. *Why don't I show people the same appreciation?*

How many times have I opened the door to let Dad in and then headed back to the computer yelling, "Just a second, I'll be right with you."

"You made my day," a good friend used to say whenever I called her at work. It seemed a bit much, but it sure made me feel good. I like to hear it but seldom say it. Maybe I should try it.

Is there is a lesson coming from the last couple of weeks? It sure seems God is giving me dog cues again.

A generous man will prosper; he who refreshes others will himself be refreshed. ~ Proverbs 11:25

Dear Lord, thank You for the kindness and warmth of our dogs. Thank You for their sweet and simple affirmation and heartfelt greetings. Thank You for their appreciation.

Open our awareness so we can practice with others some of the wonderful qualities our dogs display on a regular basis. Make it part of our routine. Help us overcome our own selfish barriers and pride to show others they are special with good human and humane random acts of kindness.

In the Master's Shadow

River walk days are always my favorite. This morning I decided to pick up the path at a remote river access site even further from the maddening crowd. Although we started our dog walk late—I felt excited.

Mickey, my silver schnauzer, who once lived along the river with a homeless master, trotted reluctantly behind me. We wound along the paved path through a half-mile of open space and full sun.

Never a sun-worshipper, I coveted the shady path beneath rows of cottonwood trees ahead. Soon our jaunt would transform to a waterfront view and cooler temperatures.

Suddenly, Mickey stopped moving—I turned around. The more I tugged his leash, and coaxed him, the more it felt like me against a fire hydrant.

"Doggonit Mick!" All four paws jammed into the ground at a 45-degree angle. His hind quarters braced into a grounded anchor. Not one of Mickey's better moments—his eyebrows knit and lips curled further toward the pavement in a classic schnauzer frown.

"We're almost to the grove of trees Mickey—then it won't be so hot." Human reasoning could not penetrate his overheated little body. He turned his head and slipped me another sideward scowl, appearing unconvinced and unimpressed I had dragged him out into hundred-degree weather.

The trees beckoned. *They're so close*. I studied Mickey—too heavy to carry today. Annoyed, I ricocheted back the direction we came.

Mickey instantly spun around and hustled ahead taking alpha position. His short silver legs swept back and forth as though pacing a clock's second hand. *How can he move so much faster than minutes before?*

Sweat dripped behind my neck from the sun's rays. I smiled and watched his little body roll like a locomotive, except the strong misalignment to his left … an injury from earlier years. True Mickey form. *He's walking in the shade … no wonder he's doing so well*. Then it hit me.

Mickey was walking dead-center in my shadow. He trotted with ease centered in the shade my figure cast in the otherwise relentless heat—relieved and renewed. We were headed home. Psalm 91:1 sprang to mind, "He who dwells in the shelter of the Most High will rest in the shadow of the Almighty."

God created us to walk beneath His protective shadow. To walk steady and confident of safety guided within the parameters of His presence.

Had I been handling the heat at work outside of God's presence? Trying to push through impossible situations apart from Him? Not praying for wisdom or walking in the ways He had revealed through His Word, through Proverbs? How long had I been treading in uncomfortable circumstances—beyond my better judgment?

I am a human master. Today I lacked wisdom and placed my desires above Mickey's best and what *he* could tolerate.

But God is not like that. He loves us fully. He will not compromise our health or sanity beyond what is good in His heavenly perspective. He will provide a way of escape. No matter how hot the pavement and daunting the journey, as long as we stay close to Him, centered under His mighty shadow of love, we can walk with assurance. Even though the path may be difficult, we will make it safely home.

Whoever dwells in the shelter of the Most High will rest in the shadow of the Almighty. I will say of the Lord, "He is my refuge and my fortress, my God, in whom I trust." ~ Psalm 91:1–2

Thank you, Lord, for reminders that we were never meant to live life apart from You and Your abiding presence, provision and protection. No matter how long our path, or how heated the journey, we trust You to bring us relief.

We trust You have set limits and times no man can extend or exploit. Thank You for the safety and the shadow of Your wings, sheltered from harm and loved..

It's a Dog, Dog, Dog, Dog World

"Is it always like this?" My high school friend squinted and grinned, amused, as she began to comprehend that invisible dog undercurrent after only a few moments of sitting in a public place with my dogs. We relished bites of warm bagels underneath a large patio umbrella at one of my favorite outdoor cafes in the afternoon fall sun.

An elegant woman in an A-line suit and coiffed hair had just left, after dropping by for a few minutes of dog conversation. It started when she bee-lined out of the jewelry shop, package in hand, and after spotting Benji, darted straight to our table. Benji and Sam lay underneath us as we ate, joined to the table and chairs by their leashes. The elegant woman eyed Benji, head to stump, with a distinct electric smile. She showed great admiration for Benji—who did not respond. He remained silent and guarded in his tense *achtung* (attention) schnauzer stance throughout her gentle cajoling.

"Oh, I thought he was a puppy!" She exclaimed, disappointed at each retreat to her advance.

"I have two schnauzers at home." Her eyes shone into mine. It was obvious she liked me—just for owning a schnauzer.

As soon as she left, a man strode toward us in tall blue jeans. He brashly approached Sammy—hand out—and patted his head while talking to all of us. "Hi boy, so you're a golden retriever." He winked at Sam. Sammy blinked back.

"No, he's a yellow Lab."

"Yeah, I had a retriever just like him once!" He continued stroking Sam's head speaking to him through dancing eyes. Sam returned the gaze with equal ardor, until the man spun on his heels and took off, thanking me for his magical moment.

I turned back to my friend and tried to answer her last question. Just then, a lady approached, squatted down, looked over Benji *and* Sam, and shared her observations of them…with them. They seemed to like the, "Oh, aren't you handsome?" and, "What a lovely boy you are," as she patted both of them. She showed no favoritism toward little or big.

"Yes, dogs are magnets. There is a whole dog world around us that we find when we take our dogs out. They're everywhere." I lifted my eyes, not looking at the lady behind me, because I wanted to visit with my friend—not engage in dog chit-chat. We had a few uninterrupted sentences when Sam started barking. And barking.

As soon as Benji started, I glanced behind me. A blond boy, no taller than four feet, squinted his eyes and squeezed raspberries from his tightly pursed lips at the table next to ours. It was tike-size taunting testosterone, accompanied by a baby sister in a stroller and tired looking Mama.

"Can he pet them?" the mom pleaded. What's a dog Ma to do? Brighten the corner where we are, letting the human family visit our furry family. It was a brief and friendly encounter. The dogs let the taunting tike touch them and laugh.

My friend still shook her head. "I've never seen anything like this."

"That's because you have a cat. Now you see how dogs can change your life and open up a silent world all around us into a mobile amusement park. We're talking to everyone we meet like *Alice in Wonderland*. Dogs are the key to the world with a door like the one Alice stepped through. Sitting in a public place becomes a new experience with the dogs. Just bringing them along—like Tweedle Dee and Tweedle Dum—draws a cast of characters on the daily stage of life I wouldn't know existed."

So, that day my friend became a best supporting actress in our dog drama. And she will never forget the performance. She will always remember this experience, because we were all together.

As water reflects a face, so a man's heart reflects the man. ~ Proverbs 27:19

Thank You, Lord, for the blessing the dogs are in creating humor and lighthearted communication with so many strangers. For breaking down the walls of distrust and apathy between people in our community and bringing us together in our common love of dogs.

I am grateful for those who share time with us and themselves discover the public world of dog lovers.

I am Mickey, Not Maude

Swooping Mickey up from his tumble, I cradled him like a baby and walked across the yard. I gazed into the blank little eyes staring up at me half-dazed, as dull as black marbles. He had no idea why he couldn't do something his little friend Maude could do. Maude's dour gray feline coat matched Mickey's. That is about all they had in common.

"You can't do that, Mickey!" I rocked him back and forth in my arms. "Maude can do it, but you can't," I explained, looking into the long lashes, hiding his grumpy glare.

He had followed Maude onto a retaining wall. I looked up just in time to see him looking down at the pavement from a three-foot perch, but my jump-start wasn't quick enough to reach him in time. Sure enough, I watched him take a step and fall down with a yelp. I hoped his legs hadn't fractured—he already limped enough from arthritis.

A little wobbly, he took a few steps and stopped, confused. That's when I arrived—the first responder. Interestingly enough, Maude could leap off a five-foot car or a six-foot fence without any problem. But Mickey's vertical was maybe five inches.

Sometimes in life I think I can do something, like run farther than I can or do more than is possible in a day. I see friends around me doing it. Why can't I?

It's just the way God made me. I thought about my words to Mickey—words I need to heed myself.

Start slowing down, I thought. Think about what I'm doing. Stop taking big steps of ambition that drive me to crash from sleep deprivation and take the little steps and smaller goals that I can do—that suit my ability.

Mickey's little legs are a good reminder for me. So is admiring Maude when she's poised to leap—grace beautiful to behold. It's great Mick and I appreciate her agility, as long as we realize we are not cut from the same mold.

But by the grace of God I am what I am, and his grace toward me was not in vain.

~ 1 Corinthians 15:10 (RSV)

God Grant me the serenity to accept the things I cannot change, courage to change the things I can, and the wisdom to know the difference.

~ The Serenity Prayer, Reinhold Niebuhr

Expand Your Territory

Mickey's little body froze, his eyes riveted to the hole in our fence. His small stump of a tail moved at half the beat of his escalating bark. A black nose pressed through the oval from the other side—nostrils flaring.

"Who's boss of this backyard?" I chuckled to myself.

Mick's pitch increased as I peered through a crack between boards. The large shepherd's tail swung back and forth as his deeper barks echoed into our side yard. I breathed a sigh of relief. No need to rescue Mick without a sign of an old board breaking loose.

How rough and tough my little dog seems. I smiled. Either he has a good self-image or he doesn't know just how big his enemy really is. Or, it doesn't make a difference! He postured himself for a fight.

Mickey has the right to bark because this is his backyard and he is stating his case. He has the right to roam around his own backyard without fear and provocation. My little fido knows what is his to defend and enjoy.

Mickey's courage revealed how easily I can lose my peace and allow fear to invade my mind. Fear blocks a wellspring of good will, fresh thoughts and positive experiences that a flourishing mind, like a well-watered garden—inspires. Fear, an intrepid enemy, must be identified, released and removed.

I think I'll see if my coworker would like to have lunch with me, I will consider.

That may not be a good idea—getting too close outside of the workplace, creeps the next thought, like a fearful vine overshadowing a good thought and keeping me from branching out.

I think I'll take a walk in this new neighborhood, I'll muse while driving around a nice area.

Trailing that idea seed is another weed. *Well, if I park my car here, someone may try to steal something when I'm out of sight.*

Far too often, I have thoughts that would expand my borders, only to deal with discouraging doubts that hem me in the next instant.

"Go for it, Mickey" I encouraged my brave dog. *Go for it, Dee,* I encouraged myself. Life is my backyard. God gave it to me.

Jabez called out to the God of Israel, "Oh, that you would bless me and enlarge my territory! Let your hand be with me, and keep me from harm so that I will be free from pain." And God granted his request.

~ 1 Chronicles 4:10

Help me, God, to ignore the fears, big though they seem, knowing I'm safe to try new experiences. I want to devour and enjoy all of the territories You have placed before my little life, the world You have given me to explore.

Triggers

For me, dog walks are my chance to chat with friends who live far away. This morning my friend interrupted our phone conversation as she walked her Bichon puppy. "Whose dog is that?"

A male voice droned in the background.

"Oh," she responded, "it's friendly—you've seen it before?" She then resumed her chat with me on the phone, her voice lowering an octave. "There was a dog sitting out on the porch unleashed and no owner around. Now I understand why you got so upset, when we were camping last summer, with the man who refused to leash his large dog that attacked Benji."

"I hate it when dogs run wild."

"Me too. Especially since those coyotes snatched Mom's dog in front of her house and ran off, I'm paranoid. Strange dogs trigger me now."

Triggers, unpleasant dog memories, are with us the rest of our dog days—like it or not.

Today half a street up, I saw two tiny black and white terriers circling towards us like whirling brushes of a street cleaner. A car turned slowly and parked near them on the sidewalk. My inner alert rang: Beware!

Trouble! In seconds they swirled toward Sammy, Benji and I on our morning walk.

"Get away," I commanded, stopping my dogs, while the attackers moved toward us traversing the street spinning, yipping…and aggressive. Benji's shrieks crescendoed while Sammy's barks rustled the birds from the bushes.

Another car in the distance slowly pulled into a driveway. *Whose dogs are these? Are those the owners?*

The tiny, tea-cup terriers spun toward us even as I raised my arms to appear bigger than life and made a grotesque expression. Undaunted, they continued darting at us in attack-mode. Sam's bark deepened as his ridge rose higher. Something triggered.

Just before my inner Hulk emerged, the passenger door of the dormant car sprang open. An arm appeared. I heard some muffled words. The little dogs slowly retreated backward and hopped in. I glared at the darkened windows silhouetting two figures. Moments later the car cruised up beside me—two men inside.

The driver rolled down his window, his eyes glazed over. "Lady—"

"I try to be responsible." I scowled at them. "My big dog could have easily killed one of your little hotdogs in one bite."

An hour later a friend tried to reason, "Sammy wouldn't hurt anything."

"I don't know that!" I said. "A dog is an animal. I can't always predict his behavior, any more than mine. Sammy was upset. They were rushing in. He was defending us. If he had bit one of those little Twinkies—" I shuddered. "They would probably sue me and win."

What triggered the extent of my anger this morning? My throat felt sore as I pondered the event later sitting on our bench out front. Dog owners who have untrained animals that do not come to command, yet run loose and free are my triggers—especially if they are relentless and aggressive—little or big. "Oh, he's friendly!" assurances have backfired too many times.

Triggers transcend doggie experiences into the world of people. After my house had two attempted robberies in one week, I stopped leaving the window screens open for the delta breeze and opted for the air conditioner.

One summer night soon after, I noted whether neighbors left their windows open or closed them. How many homeowners who keep their windows shut have had break-in attempts? How many dog owners who seem unwelcoming toward strange dogs have had dog attacks?

There may be a connection between open windows and open dog owners and closed windows and closed dog owners. Hopefully we can all live together in the same world discerning we all have different responses to situations based on past experiences, and even if we want to believe all dogs are good—as much as we want to believe all people are—they are not.

Trust develops toward a strange dog on a porch, the same way it develops for a new neighbor, a new coworker, or a new family member. Slow and in time. But initially, life's past experiences trigger first impressions and first reactions, until we all become old neighbors and our dogs become the dog next door.

All a man's ways seem right to him, but the Lord weighs the heart. ~ Proverbs 21:2

Lord, please grant us patience with those who have not had the bad experiences we have, which cause us to be defensive towards their animals. Grant insight to owners who feel all in dog-world is fun and free, ignoring the concerns of other dog owners.

Help us to extend the same grace and understanding into different areas of our lives where we may encounter difficult relationships because we have different perspectives and life experiences. We all need Your love and understanding to respect each other without having to explain why we choose the boundaries we do.

Keep us from taking other's boundaries personally towards us or our dogs. We all have triggers that time can heal.

Privilege

The rustle of the vertical blinds traveled into my office from the family room where Benji brushed against them. I glanced at the clock next to my computer—11:00 a.m. Benji's breakfast was overdue.

Last week Dad gave me a freezer-burnt pot roast which I salvaged by stewing it in the crock-pot. Now, I placed the tender meat in the microwave. Benji pranced below the counter—his nose and ears twitched as his nails tapped on the laminate floor.

"This is the last of it, Benji." I pulled the tender meat apart with a fork. Benji's eyes danced. "This has been a special treat, but it won't be like this in the future." He tailgated me as I carried brunch to his eating spot and stayed until I signaled okay. His snout dove into the divine dish and disappeared.

Boy, is he going to have a hard time tomorrow! I walked away.

This is the fourth and final day for Benji to have real meat. People food. I sat down to read, only to be interrupted moments later by a little paw stroking my arm.

"No more," I said aloud. "All gone." I looked into his piercing black eyes. Maybe it wasn't such a good idea to give Benji a steady diet of such expensive food. Now he may snub his regular dog food even more than usual.

Sam, his big brother, had only a few bites of the roast as an occasional treat—but then Sam thinks *all* food is a treat. Dry or moist, old or fresh, people or dog food, even cat food—he doesn't care.

Benji is imbued with a designer dog palate. Regular dog food sits hours until he's resigned to eat it as a last resort. And now I had privileged him and he would expect it tomorrow. He grunted and I wondered how long he would wait for steak before he eats his run-of-the-dog-mill nuggets.

I wished Benji could see how dogs live in other parts of the world, like Mexico or Samoa. I still remember wincing at ribs protruding from dry mangy coats of homeless dogs roaming the streets. Even those who had owners were often malnourished. On one of our missionary trips, a friend picked sixty ticks off of a puppy that eventually died. The family barely had money to feed their children let alone buy pet medicine or vaccinate their animals.

My dogs are dogs of privilege, blessed to live in a country of privilege. Benji lingers hours before eating his dog food. He repeatedly visits his bowl halfheartedly pushing it around as if he's waiting for something tastier. Like gravy or human table morsels. But plain dog food? Reluctant, eventually he resigns himself to eat. He acts ungrateful. But I am no different if I hear of friends going out to eat a lot and I must eat at home due to my budget. How thankful am I just to have food when many children in Africa eat only once or twice a week?

I once read the biography of General William Booth, the founder of the Salvation Army. He lived among 100,000 poor in the slums of East London during the Industrial Age. There were no child labor laws, human trafficking abounded, and he watched toddlers climb stepstools and drink whiskey in dingy bars.

A beam of compassion swept the dirt of despair as Booth proclaimed the gospel street by street. Lives reversed from spiral decline. Bands of derelicts and alcoholics transformed to an "army" equipped with purpose and hope. Booth rallied for child labor laws and better working conditions. His vision spread and he sent missionaries to help the downtrodden in India and beyond.

Invitations from royal courts throughout Europe poured in as he became known for his work in London and abroad protecting the innocent and helping the poorest of the poor. He would politely decline their sumptuous palace breakfasts preferring oatmeal, his normal diet. He didn't want to spoil himself. Soon he would return to his daily life among the impoverished.

Tomorrow, Benji may be upset with me and refuse his food. But he has all that he needs to live a good life, and I do too. Normal is enough. Simple is good. Maybe today I needed to be reminded—just like Benji—the good life is a privilege not a right.

Bless the Lord, O my soul, and forget not all his benefits. ~ Psalm 103:2 (KJV)

Thank You, God, for the times of plenty and the times of plain. Help me to treasure them all from Your gracious hand, and be thankful I have never lacked for anything.

Haircuts

"He's looking awfully scraggly." My nephew, David, wrinkled his nose. "He smells. Can't you smell him?"

I stuck my nose in Mickey's fur. "I can't smell a thing."

That was yesterday before taking David to school. Today, I sat on the floor trying to cut my poor pup's matted hair while he struggled to get away. As usual, I hoped to reason him into compliance.

"I was embarrassed taking you to the vet yesterday," I informed my clueless pooch. He just wriggled harder out of my left hand grip, dodging the scissors poised like a weapon in my right hand. I winced—still humbled by my apology to the vet yesterday. "I planned to bathe him." She played poker with her face.

Earlier today while throwing my laundry in the washer, the theme persisted. *My teenage nephew is more organized than I. Each time he stays, he brings his clothes to wash—like clockwork.* And for some reason, I struggled wanting to use the washer before he did—although my stuff had been sitting in the basket accumulating for days.

Now Mickey dove for the chair and peeked at me

from underneath, ready to duck and dive should his Master Scissorhands venture too close. *Yesterday I took David to get his haircut after he mowed the lawn, which also needed a trim. It seems I am barely able to maintain my environment.*

Mickey is scruffy, my lawn is the longest on our street, my dirty clothes pile is growing daily—all these facts poked at me like cue sticks from every direction to begin making adjustments—some easy steps toward change. Maintain and manage. Pick a laundry day, a lawn day, and schedule hair cut appointments for Mickey and me. Plan with diligence and mark it on the calendar. "Make a plan then work the plan," as a family member used to say.

My neighbors keep their lawns manicured and walk their dogs with pride. Some have big dogs with flowing fur that needs frequent grooming. Why do I shun those owners when my little guy's mouth is brown from food and his mustache and beard is wearing it? Wearing whatever he's been into and now reeks of. Something needs to change. *Me.*

"Mickey you'll be my indicator," I spoke decisively to my little Houdini, recaptured to the shearing area. "If I'm too busy socializing to take care of business, I'll know it by looking at you. Your beauty is my business."

Mickey pushed my hand up with his nose, and hopped away while I sat admiring his coat again...and that handsome little face with the trimmed beard. And really, it didn't even take that long.

The plans of the diligent lead to profit ...
~ Proverbs 1:5

🐾

Lord, help me to take care of myself and my dog and all the big and little things in my world that reflect order and care. Nudge me to *stop* procrastinating and make time for the non-demanding deeds I ignore on my rounds to meet the ring of the phone, the roar of work and the greater causes in life. Little things mean a lot.

Chocolate

"Hi, Mickey!"

I looked down at my curious silver mini schnauzer gazing up at me and pulled the key out of the garage-laundry room door. It was eleven o'clock and I longed for my bed. Christmas dinner at my neighbor's lasted longer than I planned.

"What are you doing?" I laughed out loud. A gift bag hung crooked around Mickey's neck by two half-loops.

"You silly guy. What have you been into?" I carefully lifted the corded handles over his head. Mickey turned and trotted off. Curious, I followed him down the hallway.

Wrappers? Loose colorful foils marked a haphazard trail to my bedroom. I collected each one and plopped on my bed clutching nineteen chocolate wrappers. I looked around. Red and green torn paper lay beside an empty truffle box. *Where did that come from?*

Mickey hopped up next to me and shoved his face near mine, panting. I scuffled his hair and laughed. Our faces were so close I could feel his breath.

"Mickey, you smell like chocolate! You little rascal—eating all this chocolate!" We sat on the bed together, each grinning, while I stroked his back, talked and half-scolded him—for a whole minute.

Suddenly a new thought wafted between my ears. *Chocolate is bad for dogs. It's poison.* The laugh intercepted, my emotions reeled to grave concern.

"Oh my gosh, Mickey, what have you done to yourself?" I glanced down the end of the hall to my roommate's den, where a pile of Christmas presents sat on the floor. She had forgotten to shut her door again.

I scrambled for the phone number of the 24-Hour Emergency Vet, dialed, and braced myself.

"How many did he eat? Were they dark or milk chocolate? How much does he weigh?" Frantic, I answered the calm, concerned woman on the other end.

"Nineteen."

"Milk."

"Sixteen pounds."

By the last answer I was shaking.

"What time?"

"I don't think it's been too long because I found one truffle still in its wrapper—number twenty. I think that's when I came home and interrupted his binge."

"Bring him in right away and we'll pump his stomach—hopefully it hasn't all absorbed. Dogs can die from chocolate. A quarter bar of baking chocolate can kill a Lab. It depends on how big they are and how much they eat—but it's good it was milk chocolate and not dark."

I cried over these words during that long twelve-mile ride to the ER vet while Mickey sat quiet and content in the backseat. I woke a few good friends on that stretch of road, desperate for prayers. His stomach was pumped, he spent the night medicated, and I brought him home the next day.

Like Mickey, we can also get into trouble real fast, blindsided by ease or pleasure, unable to see where we are thoughtlessly heading. Sometimes it takes a while to notice the danger signs for others as well as ourselves.

We can amble into a crisis and not recognize it at first. I have laughed with friends burgeoning into hoarders as their home and garage space disappears, swallowed by stuff. I've listened to others' difficulties over $5 cups of specialty coffee—a daily routine despite mounting debt. Sat by, removed and unencumbered, as laundry and dishes overtook someone's sanctuary beyond sanitary, disconnected from their precarious slide into chaos. Reality hits. Things are bad and not getting better.

Everyone needs a wise friend to listen, give feedback, and possibly even use their hands as burden-bearers. Lack of self-control may necessitate some intervention from others. The time is never convenient, but problems need to be addressed and shared by someone—family or friend, a professional or community of those who care. What would stop us from prayerfully addressing a topic of concern for someone we care about?

Sometimes we have our own personal crisis. We overload on chocolate, literally. We are laughing about pants we can't fit into anymore and we've already given away clothes that were a size smaller last year. We know that our budget is stretched and our knees hurt.

Maybe we would exchange whining and apprehension for new habits if we perceived where this path leads. The limitations—the quality of life we would like to enjoy—are they worth the passing pleasure of tasting a few more chocolates?

We are all susceptible to incrementalism. What is pleasurable and safe at one, can quickly multiply to toxic—lethal to our lives or lifestyle—in a few short steps.

One glass of wine to relax after a hard day at work turns to three. One beer to socialize becomes a six-pack. One outfit results in a new fall wardrobe. One lottery ticket—why not ten and a trip to the Casino? Temptation lurks with accessibility.

Mickey is still blissfully ignorant about his binge night. Given one chocolate or ten, he would still beg for another. When I left him at the vet hospital the night they saved his life—he stood and frowned at me. I learned a hard lesson about chocolate. It needs to be stored out of sight and far from the reach of any dogs in my house. And maybe, it's not a bad idea to keep it out of the kitchen—except in small quantities—from me.

The wise man looks ahead. The fool attempts to fool himself and won't face facts. ~ Proverbs 14:8 (TLB)

Thank You, Lord, for the gift of wisdom which You give us daily when we ask. Help us to know how to help when seeing a friend's predicament and how to change when we must acknowledge our own.

Please give us the strength and energy to help our friends and ourselves face reality with hope. Guide us to a practical plan for a more satisfying life today and a promising tomorrow.

Dog on the Loose

We walked parallel to the barbed-wire fence and stared at the motionless black Guernsey bull, whose head turned to face us. Wisps of grass dangled from his mouth as he gazed at us un-blinking. I gripped Sammy and Pepper's leashes tighter in my folded fingers. It seemed the bull wasn't expecting company on his country road at 6:30 a.m.

We love walking the winding pavement and rolling oak-studded countryside of the Lincoln foothills when visiting Dad. His immediate area remained pristine and somewhat protected from the surrounding developers when it was the fastest growing in California.

Lost in thought, we ambled down the lane. *It's still peaceful here—after thirty years these roads resemble those of my adolescence.* The 250 acres of land directly across from Dad's remain serene and free of houses after old Wally died at 87. His ranch, complete with obsidian arrowheads and large holes ground in granite for acorn crushing, portray a pale reminder of the Maidu tribes that lived here long ago.

Suddenly, a truck swerved to a halt ten feet away and a young man leaned out his window, "Be careful, there's a loose dog up the road." He grinned beneath his baseball hat. "I thought I'd warn you so you could take another way."

"What kind of dog?" I gripped Sam's leash.

"It's a big red dog. Doesn't have a collar." He paused. "I'd go another direction."

"Well the house I'm going to is right up the road." I pointed straight and eyed the back of his clean pick-up. I just couldn't ask if he might give us a ride back to my dad's house. He didn't offer. Maybe he was afraid that Sam, my one hundred plus pounds of field Lab, might scratch his spotless truck.

"What should I do?" I asked him expecting something other than his blunt reply.

"I'd go around."

I decided to take my chances. The sun was blazing and I did not have the stamina for a marathon today. "I'll just pray," I said.

He floored the gas pedal and left while I gathered a few stones in my timid hands. I advanced with caution, not convinced I'd made the right call. *Was I testing God by avoiding the long way when I'd been warned?* I had to trust God with this sprint.

After a country block, Sammy and Pepper's heads pivoted simultaneously, like two wooden players mounted together on a foosball set, toward a house to our left. A dark auburn stud stood poised like a lion atop the driveway. He glared at us, his long tail curled up with the distinct look of an Akita or Chow. He even curled his lip, I think. No sign of his owner nearby, there were no human beings to be seen anywhere for miles around. Just me.

I prayed to God the dog would stay put and turned my head straight down the road, breaking eye contact.

Sammy and Pepper walked in a strange silence. We hurried along, me clasping the rocks in my hand and whispering prayers to God, who created dogs and cows and all the animals of paradise. I wished it was now like it was then. I could only imagine all the animal species together, walking and grazing unthreatened by each other. My relief ratio was directly proportional to the distance from the lion on the driveway. No thumping paws or growling ensued—the lion had not lurched.

I realized if we had walked here minutes earlier—when the red dog was king of the road—it could have been another story. An uneventful return home made the day's gratitude list for what had *not happened* and became another small lesson in trust.

My grace is sufficient for you, for my power is made perfect in weakness. Therefore I will boast all the more gladly about my weaknesses, so that Christ's power may rest on me.   ~ 2 Corinthians 12:9

Thank You, God, for protecting us in ways we don't even realize so many times each day. Thank You for strangers that care. Help us look out for others we pass by today, who may need our awareness, our concern or our interception. And most of all thank You for reminding us again that Your grace is sufficient for not only for the marathons in life but also the sprints.

Bone Wars

"No, no, no, Pepperoni." I raised my voice as the teeny black-and-silver fur ball hopped and jumped, growled and snatched the bone from his brother—a new-toothed, yellow-hulk puppy. Both scurried and tumbled on the living room carpet.

God please don't let them take an eye out, I thought as they snapped at each other, the little teeth and then the big teeth—like alligator chops.

Mouths and bones—first thing in the morning and they were at it again! I envisioned a terrific duo, not dramatic dueling, when I added baby Pepper to our house, the house that Sammy had lived in all of his five months.

Bone wars. One wanting what the other had. I gave them each their own bone. No sooner had I left a small bone in front of the tiny tike and a big bone in front of the big (really big) brother and a leap and a yelp later, it started all over! The tiny tike wanted the big bone. *This is wasting my time again*, I fumed hotter than my tea.

I plopped down between my great big yellow Lab and tiny miniature schnauzer on the floor, clutching my read, *Purpose Driven Life*. Lately, my whole purpose seemed wasted, serving as peacemaker between these walls. Is this any way to spend valuable time?

Good boys. I patted each one, my body perched in a perfect visual-field block position of each dog's chew object. They seemed to be content for the moment.

I patted their heads again saying, "Good boys. You each have *your own*. You each play with *your own*." The little black nose bobbed above his bone busily while the big pink nose moved from side to side with each powerful grind.

Maybe there was a purpose in this. Why is it that sometimes *our own* isn't good enough? We want the other person's floors, car, work description or assignment. Sometimes I even wish I ordered what the other person chose at the restaurant! Isn't this what I fight daily within myself even as my pups exhibit their outward display of discontent and envy? Sure, the bones were shaped a little different and maybe even had a different flavor in the rawhide but they were the same stuff.

Yesterday I interviewed for another job. I must leave it in God's hands and thank Him for what He gives me, even now, before I get it.

These last few moments Pepper lay still, bent around his ragged piece of dog jerky. I watched Sammy fixated on the white chew in his mouth. Right now they owned their own bone. I leaned back against the mattress. Maybe for now I could be content with what is before me also. Maybe I could enjoy today.

Love your neighbor as yourself. If you keep on biting and devouring each other, watch out or you will be destroyed by each other. ~ Galatians 5:14–15

God, I am grateful there is no greater gift than the present. Help me to be satisfied with my daily bread and to stop wanting what You have given my neighbor. Thank You for the abundant provision in my life, and keep me focused on what You have put in front of me to digest and chew on today.

Mickey's Magic Meatball

The moment I laid eyes on Mickey's frazzled face, following his annual teeth cleaning and extractions, I knew something was wrong. All day I'd felt uneasy, haunted by a former roommate's story about her Lab who died under general anesthesia while having a simple procedure. The forebodings fueled my mind—now, I didn't like this picture.

"Eight teeth!" I alarmed the substitute vet who reported the extractions—the same woman who scolded me for not brushing his teeth every day. I rescued Mickey from his doggie dream diet. He survived on people food years before I received him and began the battle for his teeth.

"No, he doesn't need pain pills, he'll be fine, just let him sleep," she too easily reassured me, answering my questions brusquely, before shooing us out to close shop.

I reluctantly drove him home. Two hours later, Mickey was still listless and shaking, eerily awake and moaning in a penetrating pathetic way I'd never heard. It was late, but before long we headed for the nearest emergency vet hospital.

Mickey lay quietly as the husky thoughtful vet checked his eyes with a light and examined his mouth, giving him a gentle and thorough assessment. "He's in pain," he stated looking up at me and motioning the young girl standing near the exam table.

She left the room and reappeared with a smile and a treat, "Here's a little meatball for Mickey," she said sweetly. The pony-tailed vet assistant had fashioned a one-inch meatball around a little white pill from the can food on the shelf.

For the first time all day, Mickey's ears perked up and his dull eyes brightened. He chewed softly on the meatball and laid his little head back down to rest. I felt more at ease, but stiffened with a new resolve, *Mickey's never having general anesthesia again. He's just too old.* I continued stroking my pet's blood tinged fur and listening to his moans. I talked to God, my eyes burning, "Lord, I just don't feel like I'm ready to lose Mickey yet."

As though God were reminding me of His goodness and wisdom, I suddenly remembered years before walking with my mom outside the Kaiser Hospital doors, from visiting my critically ill stepdad in ICU.

"I'm not ready," Mom's hoarse voice trembled as she gripped my hand. "I don't know what I'll do if Ed dies." For a moment I was silent, but I felt unusually peaceful.

Pacing her rapid steps, I answered confidently, "Don't worry Mom, he isn't going to die. I don't know why, but I feel this isn't his time yet."

And it wasn't. But six years later, when my stepdad did not survive the ICU, my mom handled his death very well. She had a strength and peace only God could give her.

So now, choking back the tears, I reaffirmed my trust in God's faithfulness. He would never lead me where His grace could not keep me. And Mickey.

"It's amazing what a meatball can do!" The vet, his assistants and I laughed in agreement, as Mickey aroused, stood on his feet and begged for another meatball. He was back in form—acting like his old dumpster-diver self.

"I'll buy two of those cans from you," I laughed, gathering my hungry pet in my arms and heading out the door. Relief and gratitude flooded me as we drove home.

My times are in your hands.　　　　～ Psalm 31:15

Thank you, God, for bracing me for unexpected trials and keeping my emotions intact. Help me to use my head and trust you to guide me when I'm not sure what to do. Lead me to wise people and kind spirits. I know I can trust you with all the events of life both for me and my dog.

Feed My Need

When Sammy wants food he barks, and barks and barks. He won't quit barking at me until I feed him. He is *assertive.*

I pick Benji's bowl from off the floor when he's munched some nuggets and left, so Sammy can't reach it. Often, I forget to set the bowl back down. Later, when Benji wants food and he is hungry—he tears things apart—my rug, pillow, and other forbidden items. His destructive behavior alerts me he is hungry and wants to eat. He is *passive-aggressive.*

If he's *really* hungry and I haven't noticed torn items, he nips my ankles with his teeth, amidst *"grrrr's"* he chomps down enough to get an *"ooww"*! It hurts. It moves me to action—to take care of his needs. He is direct and *aggressive.* I respond to the pain and he directs my attention to his empty bowl.

When Mr. Gill is hungry he floats up from the bottom of the fish bowl and floats quietly at the top. It seems he hopes I will see him and remember his little energy pellets that bob on the surface of the water. He is *passive.*

We all have ways to let people around us know we have needs—very real needs. Sometimes we are downright annoying by how we express our needs. Sometimes, we are destructive by our demanding tone and actions trying to get legitimate attention. Other times we are too passive which frustrates others...and doesn't help us. How can we change our behavior to better express our needs to each other?

It seems we can always improve our delivery. It's hard to get it perfect. Sometimes our delivery is way too forceful, like Sam. "Do this for me now!" rather than a gentle, patient approach and politely asking, "When you have a moment, would you please help me out?"

Or like Mr.Gill we sit quietly hoping someone will notice we are hungry—when we are starving! Our visibility is going down a notch every day. *Need a little attention over here if you get your head out of the computer room and all the paperwork. If you happen to look up?*

We may stack up resentment at someone's oversight. "Can't you tell I need this done? Well, maybe now that that I broke it and cut myself and it's going to cost more money—you'll help me sooner when I ask you—you'll pay more attention next time!" Guilting others and playing victim, shaming or blaming, doesn't substitute for asking in a direct, polite manner for what we need from them. This also allows them to feel valuable to us and purposeful as helpers and givers.

I wish I could direct my pets to better behaviors that work for all of us. Maybe if Sam would give one bark and a nudge, instead of whining and flipping his snout on my arm like a rotorooter. Or, if Benji brought my glasses over dangling in his mouth alerting me he's about to go on a rampage if something doesn't happen here soon to get my attention—before he rips them up. Or bite into my ankle. And if Mr.Gill swam around in his jar a bit so I remember he's around… it would help.

I forget to pray, to ask God for what I need—and then trust Him and His goodness as I wait for provision. Every day I hope to remember to ask God to give me *this day* my *daily* bread," as Jesus taught. To be quick to release, let go, of heightened frantic feelings… and relax. Approach God first—not my unsuspecting friends. Maybe, I wouldn't come across so self-centered and demanding to others, when I'm overwhelmed by tasks undone and my spiraling emotions. But, everyday my pets have that realization too, as they look to me to provide what they can't.

Maybe I'll be more understanding when they come off aggressive, destructive or passive, and walk into the world of people with the same insight and patience. Maybe God and others will continue to show understanding toward me when I'm demanding, frantic, pesky or withdrawn when expressing my own needs. After all, you can't understand a dog until you walk in his paws. Somehow, I'll get there.

🐾

Give us today our daily bread.   ~ Matthew 6:11

🐾

Dear God, forgive me for the times I have allowed my emotions to barrage other's time and space when I am feeling needy. Grant me grace to assert my needs with diplomacy and kindness when asking others for help. Cause me to consider the pressures and pulls of their lives while I am trying to manage mine.

Help me trust You so I can maintain peace and maturity in my daily efforts to conquer hurdles and challenges. Strengthen me to accomplish the tasks You have assigned for the day, without causing undue stress on myself or others. If my goals are not met today, I trust it wasn't the time yet. When the time comes to cross that bridge—You will provide—because You love me..

Hills

When I lived around the corner from a protected marshland, the most wonderful moments were watching my muscular black Lab, Hannah, run free. Here lay untouched open fields imbued with a beautiful, trickling, spring bordered by tall cottontails. In the middle of suburbia I felt like Alice stepping through the looking glass.

I used to sing a little song as we walked toward that field, happy Hannah would be able to unleash her endless supply of energy. As she vaulted after one jackrabbit—another popped up intercepting the trail of the first. She'd spin, flip and ricochet, barreling after the spindly grey-eared mammals slowed only by the sudden appearance of another creature ... perhaps a snake or a gopher hole.

Sometimes she'd stop abruptly—her front paws pedaling like a shovel on steroids. In moments, Hannah's torso could vanish ... eclipsed by her protruding bottom next to a growing mound of dirt.

Hannah never seemed to bother the red-winged blackbirds perched like sentries atop the stalks lining the creek. But she would chase other birds and jump in the air far from their tiny claws.

I studied her actions perched atop a hill under a small tree providing shade on the path where I released her. There I read and prayed, frequently checking on Hannah to see what she was up to, amused and pleased by her curiosity and pleasure.

Those times with Hannah reminded me of similar experiences as a child in Redwood City, off Brewster Avenue where my father grew up. My grandparents built their house at the bottom of a small steep hill. It was the hill where Dad met an old timer who taught him the art of picking mushrooms as a child. He carried them home to my delighted German grandma for her stews during the Depression. My brothers and I scoured that hill for wildflowers as elementary school children and gathered bouquets to offer our grateful mother as a gift.

In my teen years, the flowers from the hill vanished under the homes, driveways and manicured landscaping that covered every last inch.

But still, I climbed the winding streets and found a bush to sit under, tucked up my knees and wrote in my journal. As a new believer I imagined what it was like to be God gazing down on the miles of streets with the sparkling San Francisco Bay in the distance.

I watched people riding bicycles, walking alone, and parents holding their children's hands as they strolled along. Multiple turquoise shapes speckled the landscape as I surveyed the city, surprised by the number of backyard pools hidden from the roads.

I pretended to have God's relational heart and how it must feel to have one of those people acknowledge and speak to me. It felt amazing. I wondered how it would feel to be the person, the small distant figure crossing the street, to know God was watching them and cared for their safety—just as I was experiencing a new relationship with a loving God who cared about me.

Although it was another field and a small berm, again a deep impression from my youth revived with Hannah.

"Hannah, Hannah!" when it was time to go home, I would stand up so she could see me. Immediately she looked up to me from wherever her position in the field, even if she did not stop her current preoccupation—always aware she was not alone.

Sometimes, even when I didn't call Hannah, she would stop what she was doing and look up to where I sat on the hill. The same spot I always sat. Hannah always knew where to look to find me, just like we know to look up to find God.

O Lord, you have searched me and you know me. You know when I sit and when I rise, you perceive my thoughts from afar. You discern my going out and my lying down; you are familiar with all my ways.

~ Psalm 139:1–3

Lord, thank you for watching over me, taking pleasure in me and delighting in me. Keep me aware of your presence when I work and when I play, when I am moving with intention or caught up in my surroundings distracted, wandering or obsessed. You know my nature and you accept me. Keep me mindful to whisper words of love and thanks to you in my daily moments.

It's the Fight in the Dog

"Come on, Little One. Come on, Shorty and Smiley. Come on, Puppy." We called to the canine motley crew we'd grown to love while volunteering at the Women's Rehab tucked away in Northern Mexico.

Four dogs comprised the present pets on the premises. Smiley, the medium-built black dog with an immense overbite that earned him the nickname. Shorty, the large orange and yellow dog that had six-inch legs to hold his overstuffed, overly affectionate frame. Puppy, a spry wiry white-and-black Jack Russell terrier mix, with dirt cling-ons covering his matted coat and small frame. And finally, Little One, a black-haired sturdy-built mutt with a shriveled right leg tucked up useless in front of him. Since it couldn't bear weight he simply carried it around working his other three paws, leaving a signature track on the ground wherever he trod.

This early morning, it was especially wonderful to walk this dusty arid road. Strange bird calls drifted through the dawn. We felt safe escorted by our small band of frolicking *perros* (dogs)—our personal body guard team. They scurried around us, creating an undeniable energy force-field, eying each other, then us, seeming to anticipate the journey ahead up the scrub brush mountain.

We grinned at each other slowing our jog by the place where the sows wallowed in their favorite element. Barbed-wire fences outlined some of the small rancherias, broken wooden posts lined others. A large greenhouse spanned the borders of one farm, housing a colorful flower nursery. Rows of cactus crops standing at attention like dutiful green soldiers armed with spindly shoots, occupied another.

Every property along the rocky dirt road seemed to have dogs—dogs that barked or howled, protecting their territory. Eventually, we passed an unfenced property marked by posts and guarded by two frowning pit bulls. My heart quickened as they charged toward us from the porch. I feared for the motley crew thinking they were no match for these ultimate fighters of the dog world.

As we prayed for safety, our fabulous four grunted in unison. They scuffled together to form a sort of haphazard line of defense and ran past the posts into the pit bull's zone. We stopped and stared transfixed like we were watching the fourth down of the final play in a Superdog Bowl. Growls and yips, barks and *rrr*'s synchronized to a thunderous fortissimo—the perfect background stanza for the peak of this early-morning dog drama.

Then…silence. No bites. No blood. The pit bulls retreated from the daunting defensive line. They back-stepped while facing our fearsome foursome— who stood together as one cohesive force—not to be reckoned with. We all guffawed and praised our team, literally the underdogs. Laughing and cavorting we hustled down the brown bumpy road in high spirits after all our defenders joined us, or so we thought. Suddenly we noticed one was missing. We stopped.

Where was Little One? Looking back we saw him. Little One stood alone—still in the big dogs' yard. He held up his lame front right leg and faced them squarely eye-to-eye, barking ferociously while moving further into their territory.

Finally, the two pit bulls turned around and trotted all the way back to the porch. I couldn't believe it! As we called Little One he took a few more steps toward the sullen-faced foes a good dozen feet on their side of the wooden fence. Only after seconds elapsed with the pits quiet and sequestered, did he spin around and step-hop toward us. His head high, and face calm, he wobbled down the road towing his lame foot, sauntering alongside his amigos like nothing unusual had happened.

How come Little One had no fear? Why didn't he know he was the least likely to take on two big dogs?

I thought about a story my dad relayed from his youth. He reminisced about an old high school football coach's lecture to the young players, one he would never forget. "Never give up, especially when you feel you have nothing left to give. There's always a reserve there. Whenever you think you're on your last leg— you're not. There is always plenty more left."

There are times we feel tired or inadequate to stand against the forces in life that can seem to defeat us. Financial. Mental. Physical. Social. Spiritual. We all have some area we feel depleted in. Less than. It seems we don't have what it takes—we are missing something everyone around us seems to have. The question is, especially if it's true—are we letting what we don't have determine what we do have? Is our lack dictating who we are and what we are capable of? How can we change this picture?

Just as Little One realized his potential by focusing on his strengths—three working legs, rather than the "baggage leg"—the one that seemed to have no purpose other than to weigh him down—so we must stop making excuses for our personal handicaps. Instead, like Little One, we can realize our reserve and work with what we have going for us. One leg down—*no problema.*

Man looks at the outward appearance, but the Lord looks at the heart. ~ 1 Samuel 16:7

Lord, open the eyes of our hearts so we view challenges as opportunities to display Your strength in overcoming what we perceived to be shortcomings and handicaps in life. It's not the dog in the fight; it's the fight in the dog. May we see people as You see us.

Possibly physically impaired—but whole-spirited.

Help us to face our battles leaning on Your strength and our legs.

Blast from the Past

Recently I concluded, *it's easier the second time around*, after recalling ignorant moments as a "new dog mom." I remember how difficult it was for me the first week with Hannah, a Lab/Rottweiler mix I took in twelve years ago.

"Can anyone take this sweet dog?" Steve, the ER charge nurse, pleaded all night with the staff nurses on behalf of the collarless gangly pup who had wandered through our hospital Emergency Room. My heart pounded a little harder each time he made the rounds through the different areas of our large urban hospital. Everyone seemed to have an excuse.

"I have a dog."

"I don't have a place to keep it."

"My wife will kill me."

"My cat will kill it."

My coworkers had good reasons—unlike me. I simply had not had a dog in twenty years of single bliss and did not want to be tied down. All eyes turned toward me, and then the charge nurse zeroed in with intense effect, "So I don't have to take her to the pound in the morning."

Reluctantly I ended up with her and became afraid of her. At nine months old, she was sixty pounds of solid muscle—stronger than me. I was startled and grabbed my blankets when she woke me up in the middle of the night barking and making strange noises. I decided someone else would be a better candidate by the second night and so began looking for a new home immediately. Someone else needed to take her—before she bit me.

One of the docs questioned, "Why do you want to give her up?"

"She makes this deep sound from the bottom of her throat and wakes me up at 2:00 a.m. I look at her and she's standing at the end of my bed with her head staring straight at me and eyes aglow and making those noises." It really frightened me the first few times that happened.

"Oh she just wants to play!" she assured me with a smile. I was surprised.

"Well, I'm afraid she's going to bite me." I defended my crumbling case.

"No." She laughed. "That's just the way they talk to you." Given the information, my fears lessened. The next night she barked, I tossed her a toy and kept her.

Sammy became my next big dog after Hannah. A hundred and twenty pounds of burning love started out biting as a twenty pound puppy. I decided he was difficult to train because he kept biting me, no matter how many times I taught him, "No bite." That is, until I gained perspective from my patient.

"My dog gives me love bites every day," the experienced Lab owner boasted when I talked with him in the recovery room about my yellow Lab pup.

"I thought he was being disobedient," I had told my patient, explaining how I'm teaching him not to bite.

"There's a difference between biting and love bites," he explained. "Biting is intentional and you would know it because it would hurt. Love bites are gestures of affection."

"Oh," I said with a new awareness, thanking God for the people he brings across my path. I stopped scolding Sammy and to this day, he bites me *and* slurps my cheek when he can get to it.

And so we learn in life, as we grow in experience and awareness, how to live with different animals and what their non-verbal's mean. It is much like how we learn to live with different people. And usually, it's at the expense of another dog, another kid, another friend or significant-other, that we have learned the things we now know—understanding that helps us to care, respond, and live with those around us with more acceptance.

He who gets wisdom loves his own soul; he who cherishes understanding prospers. ~ Proverbs 19:8

Thank You, Lord, for those in my past, those You placed in my life to learn from. Thank You for the lessons taught, the growth and wisdom You gave me through the struggles and often misguided efforts done in my ignorance.

Help me move beyond the regret and mistakes I've made and move into the grace of growth You've given me now. May all my yesterdays be used for good today for those with me now, and bless those that I learned from the hard way, for their patience.

Dogs Teach

Dogs teach us to live, they teach us to die,
They free us to laugh, they free us to cry.
They teach us to play, no matter the weather,
The fun comes in doing and being together.

They propel us to work, when we don't want to go,
To provide food and water, fresh in their bowl.
Meals taste better when shared from a plate,
If you don't come when called, at least show up late.

They model persistence regardless of pain,
And to learn from correction is better than shame.
Don't judge by appearance, friends have to earn trust,
Though biting's forbidden, bark if you must.

Keep a positive outlook and always forgive,
When we share daily life, it's the best way to live.
If you care then express it, through kisses and rubs,
We're all made for affection; we're created to love.

Five O'Clock and All is Well

I cupped Sam's large yellow head in my hands. "Sam is afraid Mom is going to forget to feed him." He squinted and smiled. Of course, he was satiated having just gobbled down the big blue bowl of dinner ten minutes ago.

"You funny boy." I gently moved his face from side to side. His eyes remained shut, much more relaxed now that he had eaten.

"Do you think I could ever forget to feed my Sam?"

This evening, as soon as my tires hit the driveway and I parked the car, his barks boomed from the garage and continued as I entered through the front door of the house. I looked at the clock. It was 4:53 p.m. Sam knows his dinner time is five o'clock, give or take a few minutes. He might have been a bit worried I was going to be late getting home. His barking stopped when I entered the garage via the house door. He pranced around his food bags, totally uninterested in a quick hug.

Tonight I realize I'm a lot like Sam. I can go through times where I fear God is not going to provide for me. I wonder what God thinks when my prayers become as rapid and repetitive as a record skipping on a turntable.

He knows, "Dee is getting a little anxious though she has never gone without."

He doesn't make me wait until five—like I don't make Sam wait. I fed him five minutes before five. I'm not out to test him. Sometimes if Sam's tired or diverted, he can actually forget about the five-o'clock-on-the-dot thing. And if I'm on something else also, I may forget, but as soon as his loud reminders start, I feed him right away—he eats. We don't skip a beat. Never have.

Do I need to pester God all the time? I don't think so. But sometimes, if worry wells up and pushes aside my peace, I begin to point to my watch and bug God about my potentially empty bowl.

Earlier this year, money was flying away and sometimes I couldn't see a glimmer of wings near or far. But, I never missed a meal. In fact, at one of my leanest moments it happened to be my birthday. Friends gathered at a restaurant to celebrate, and I received amazing food gifts from Trader Joe's and gift cards redeemable at department stores or Safeway or Winco. God got me through in ways I would have never anticipated.

I had two roommates at different times, perfect times—and then the money started flying in again to roost.

But I know who lives up there in that heavenly blue. The same Creator who provides for me and Sammy and the birds of the air—who dine without care.

Therefore I tell you, do not worry about your life, what you will eat or drink; or about your body, what you will wear ... Look at the birds of the air; they do not sow or reap or store away in barns, and yet your heavenly Father feeds them. Are you not much more valuable that they? Who of you by worrying can add a single hour to his life? ~ Matthew 6:25–27

Thank You, Lord, for providing our daily needs and the meals on our plates. Thank You for the money to feed our pets and also the knowledge that You will continue to watch over us, just as You do the birds in the air.

Surrender

"Sammy, sit." I snapped my fingers and pointed at my eight-month-old, Jolly-Giant Lab. He had suddenly lunged at laser speed toward Pepper, his pint-size terrier brother…who sat on my lap. Defiant, Sam tugged his new puppy schnauzer's small silver-and-black ear, a possible repay for Pepper's little teeth frequently anchored in Sammy's dangling yellow ear-lobes. Now, Sam snapped and wrinkled his nose at me.

"Don't let them snap at you, ever!" The voice of the PetSmart instructor reverberated like an echo chamber. "They are like children." I set Pepper down and deftly sat on Sammy. Pushing my palms on his pink *schnozzle*, I pressed his mouth to the floor until he relaxed like a sheep being sheared.

A surge of pride in the timeliness of that teachable moment backfired as soon as I stood up and turned around. Pint-size Pepper had squatted and shot little brown pellets on the carpet runner—his doggie training paper just two feet away.

Teachable moments can appear at the most inconvenient times—*now* was the time to make an impression.

"Pepper, go potty on the paper." I swept up the two pounder deftly in a one-handed, under-the-belly transfer to the pad, using a firm, but sweet, voice.

Foiled again. *If only I could watch him like a hawk for this potty-training process the way Mom does when I leave him for Nona's doggie daycare*. Mom has the uncanny instinct to intervene before an accident occurs. Not me…distracted this time, because Sammy needed attention. My dog training felt like a ping pong game and I was losing to the dogs.

Frustrated, I felt hot inside. *Let it go*. I could hear the little voice inside me growing louder. *Let* go*! Identify the crazies*. Already struggling to order my day, I'd lapsed further behind my to-do list with these dog distractions. *Haven't read the chapter for school, haven't done my stretches or walked yet. I haven't even had a chance to refill my coffee cup*.

The day was not progressing, the dogs were not cooperating with me, nor were they getting along with each other. The familiar tune of unrealistic expectations felt similar to yesterday at work. *What is the lesson God?* I compared mornings.

Yesterday my patient was unusually slow getting ready in pre-op. He arrived late and then talked between each methodical movement to change from street clothes to his patient gown. The anesthesiologist, Ken, hung around our gurney pre-op area trying to edge his patient interviews into the nurses' patient preparations. He must have noted my strained expression when he asked, "Do you want me to start that IV?"

"Sure." I felt immediate relief as I continued running down tasks before the 7:10 a.m. recovery-operating room exit time. Even at this typical busy dawn, Rob's cheery, 'Hello, how are you this morning?' carried no sign of tension. Cordial and easygoing—he still matched the clock.

"It reminds me of Jesus," I reflected at the Bible study last night recounting how he shone with love and kindness. Here was a believer who mastered the moments, probably by walking in the knowledge God was over all.

"It's such a gift," I had reminisced. "I don't know how some people can do that. It's as if they have all the time in the world and they can make others feel special in spite of their goals at hand."

"Maybe they are truly surrendered to God's will," one woman responded. We all nodded. It seemed so. Maybe that was my teachable moment yesterday. To learn the grace of surrender and see how it is modeled.

I'm learning to yield my schedule to God, moment by moment, and listen. Then I'm ready to move forward with careful kindness, in gentler tone and touch, whether caring for people or nurturing pets. It is the purpose at hand—it brings fulfillment and satisfaction.

Not that we are competent of ourselves to think anything as coming from us; but our competence is from God. ~ 2 Corinthians 3:5 (RSV)

God help me learn surrender—to mentally prepare for detours before the day has started. To be ready to adjust and flow with life and others, at peace with the clock. Forgive me for trying to take control so quickly and allowing my temper to flare, forsaking kindness.

Thank you for my dogs and for the people you place before me to practice patience. I am committed to learn how to allot time for myself, and time to others becoming more aware when I have given enough for the moment. I understand the more time invested in dog training, the more I will enjoy them … and that is the reason you gave them to me.

Thank you for using my dog's teachable moments to teach me what you, my Master, so patiently wait for me to learn.

Special

One day, when I was working in the Post Anesthesia Care Unit (PACU), I ran downstairs for a quick, fifteen minute break and crossed paths with a coworker. She had just exited the operating room decked in green scrubs, blue shoe covers and a paper cap. We said passing hello's in the OR lounge as she sat down at one of the round tables and pulled a peanut butter jar toward her. I plopped down nearby.

"How are your Labs doing?" I asked from the easy chair, taking a bite out of my bagel.

"Gunner has to have surgery again next week." She looked up at me and rolled her eyes.

"Again! What happened?"

"He has hip dysplasia. The first time we noticed something wrong, he was six months old. He started limping."

"Unbelievable. He was so young?"

"Yes," she shook her head. "We did everything to prevent this from happening. Both he and his brother were from the same litter. We bought them from a breeder in Seattle who had a specialist check out all the puppies and clear them. We even have the ortho certificates." For a brief moment a transparent veil of grief shrouded her face and then disappeared.

"Wow, I'm so sorry."

"We called the breeder and let them know, but there isn't anything anyone could do. So we just work with it. We have no other choice. We're all attached to him." She described the healing process after surgery and how long it took to recover and how hard it was on Gunner. His movement was restricted and he had to stay in a crate.

Something triggered that day. Maybe I had just discharged an autistic child who was admitted for research. These children have to undergo conscious sedation to lie still for the brain scan. Or possibly I had a spina-bifida patient that morning with multiple, severe congenital malformations. I may have placed a port-o-cath needle in a quiet, tense leukemic child on the hematology-oncology service in for scheduled chemotherapy or a bone marrow biopsy. These children are beyond brave. So are their parents who stand nearby watching.

I've always admired the strength and loyalty of parents of children born with disabilities. The amazing sacrifice of their time and energy each and every day of their lives, often with little reward. They hope that these children entrusted to them are receiving the best of care in a world where they will lack so much of what most consider the "pleasures of life." I think there's a special place of honor in heaven for these parents.

Up until that day, hearing about Gunner from his doggie mom, I never considered the grief dog owners bear when their pets are born with lifetime maladies. I realized one more thing needed to be on my list of things I daily take for granted in my life—healthy dogs. It could have been my Sam Lab with the common developmental disorder inherent in his breed. Then today, I received an email from another friend that moved my heart. She and her husband's devotion to their dogs humbled me.

She wrote, "I am not sure I told you, but the doggie we adopted a couple of months ago somehow injured his back—ruptured a disc actually. He had surgery today and they removed the disc. The rupture compromised the spinal column. The neuro-surgeon said it didn't look bruised or damaged, so Lord willing, he will walk again. There is no guarantee but God knows—that is what we will live with. Please keep Schnitzel in prayer. He will be out of it for a few weeks.

Frankie is doing well, she had allergy testing done a couple of months ago and we found that she was allergic to almost everything we were feeding her: chicken, oats, eggs, wheat and milk. So now that we have her on a diet that agrees with her, she is flourishing and has quite a bit more energy. Praise God!"

Bless the Lord, O my soul; and all that is within me, bless His holy name! Bless the Lord, O my soul, and forget not all His benefits. ~ Psalm 103:1–2 (RSV)

Dear Lord, sweep over my heart and fill my mind today, with a sense of gratitude. Thank You for the health of my dogs and for my own health, wherever it is on the one-to-ten scale. The loyal hearts that shine from good pet owners in this world create a surge of joy in me—there are many.

Bless all the parents of special needs children and all the dog owners of special-needs doggies who are challenged in the daily struggle of scheduling doctor or vet appointments, medication and diets and troubleshooting any number of issues. Give them strength, God, and extra energy each day. Show me how I may help them, and remember to pray. Grant them abundant joy in seeing their children laugh, or in getting doggie kisses.

Doggie Park Day

"We're just leaving the doggie park," Carla, my friend in Nashville sounded a little out of breath over the cell.

I inhaled the sun-splashed, after-the-rain, San Francisco day as Dad and I drove through the Mission Street district and admired Kelly-green hills and fresh-washed streets.

"We had to leave because Honeybun had a couple male dogs after her and they wouldn't leave her alone." She sounded calm.

I laughed thinking of Pepper my persistent terrorizer. "Yes, I've had to leave before because my males were harassing a female."

"Well…" Carla sighed. "At least Honeybun marked her territory all over before we left, so she got it out of her system."

I grinned into the mouthpiece.

"Yep," she stated serenely, "it's a doggie-park day and now we're on our way to Petsmart."

We hung up and I looked around.

The Sunday-in-the-Park aura permeated the metropolis, and the variegated city dogs strolled eagerly around every busy corner. A scruffy Cairn terrier trotted beside her master fast-forward, full speed ahead on the sidewalk to the left of me. On the right side of the street a mixed border collie z-tracked back and forth, sliding like the arm of an old phonograph needle, off and on the walkway as his owner tugged relentlessly.

The polka-dog spotted hills of Delores Park extended onto the avenues as if there were no end to the appearance of hairy angels.

It must be Doggie Park Day all over America, just like on our European visit. Daily, people walked their dogs on cobblestone city streets and along gravel paths winding through the parks in Vienna. (A city employee scanned the streets every morning with a pooper-scooper!) And then I envisioned Eiffel Park in France. Dog owners threw Frisbees for their pets to retrieve. Other dogs frisked on the lawn circling and nudging each other while their masters greeted each other warmly in the early dawn.

So, doggie-park days burgeon worldwide for hundreds of dogs and breeds and peoples and nations.

The sense of community and contentment doggie-park days can offer is uncontested. It is a time to escape the phone, emails, finances, errands, or obligations. It is time out for us—courtesy of our dogs.

We go to watch and so we relax. We go to walk them and so we exercise. We go to socialize them and we are socialized. So blame it on meeting our dog's needs. Really, through them, God is meeting our needs to rest and recreate, to slow down and look around.

We look at the sky and we watch the seasons change. We walk on lawns instead of cement, to our lower-extremities delight, and we hug trees while finagling leashes wrapped around a dog-blessed trunk. So who really prospers? Maybe, our doggies are thinking in their masterful minds, they will take us out for people-park day, so that we can have a good time and unwind. Then we will be easier to live with and less agitated. One can only guess.

🐾

He who walks with the wise grows wise.

~ Proverbs 13:20

🐾

Thank You, Lord, for doggie-park days and the benefit we derive from getting out into the community and touching the earth again. Thank You for the opportunity to rest our minds from incessant decision-making by the minute and daily task triathlons.

Help us to realize we need to get out as much as we think we need to get our dogs out. Keep us from excuses that would deny our dogs the exercise and wonders of a walk that they need, and we really need too.

Sammy's Dreams

A spring Saturday afternoon proved to be the best day to wash my smelly, hairy, dog car—the one I shared with my dogs. My other car is a wish on the bumper. I vacuumed and sang with the garage boom box. Neighbor's lawnmowers hummed all around me.

After wheeling the shop-vac back to its resting place, I turned around. Sammy's massive head, posted on the top of his 120-pound Labrador frame, looked straight at me from the back seat of the Rav 4—his favorite spot in the world.

Stopping at his passenger door, I looked into Sammy's honey brown eyes.

"Sammy likes to dream. He's wondering where we can go." I smiled, patting him on the head, his pupils sparkling with possibilities. "But we're not going anywhere—not today, Sam." I hated to break the news, but a dog Ma has to do what a dog Ma has to do.

Even when it's hot outside he likes to climb in the car and sit, like he's going somewhere. I've talked to people who told me their dogs get sick in the car. But not Sam. No matter the winds or turns, no matter how long the drive, he's never restless. He stares at the scenery from the back seat of a moving adventure. He couldn't be happier than when he's traveling somewhere. Anywhere.

Ever since Sammy was four months old, my friend Gary and I took him to the Sierras. He made a game of flipping off the back of the cross country skis. He loved the great outdoors. I put doggie boots on, at his delicate age, and in minutes they'd be off. Six hours in the snow, and he'd be rolling in it, while we huddled during breaks on a large piece of plastic. Even today, four years later, he prefers a blizzard in the middle of the night to a Sacramento summer day. Water in any form is his signature element. After all, the classic manual for Labs is *Water Dog*.

His first time to the river I had a rude awakening. My three month old instantly paddled too far from the rocky shore and turned his little gold body around to keep his eyes on my face as the current began moving him past both of our comfort zones. He maintained steady eye contact from the water as I ran frantically up and down the ledge of a small cliff yelling, "Swim to the side," as if he knew what I was saying while I waved my arms like a crazy woman.

Sure enough, he paddled those strong Lab legs and obeyed me. Moments later, he crawled up on mother earth calm as a caterpillar. The river ran right through my heart, still racing by, while Sammy shook water drops off his little strawberry-blond coat, undaunted and safe. I marveled at the wonder of God-given instincts.

God made him that way. To love snow and water. To love riding in a car. To love adventure! So now, just as Sammy's dreaming in the backseat, I hope we can all let ourselves dream the dreams we need to—whether it's staying home and chewing on a good book, or going somewhere and being something that we've always wanted.

Sammy and I won't have an adventurous joy-ride today, and even though one ride will ruin my almost hair-free car, I like to take Sammy in the car as much as I can because I know that's what makes him happy.

That's how God is with us, planning the adventure we long for, if we just keep looking at Him, and keep our smile. Be patient and it will come. Ask Sammy.

O Lord, you have examined my heart and know everything about me. You know when I sit or stand. When far away you know my every thought. You chart the path ahead of me, and tell me where to stop and rest. Every moment, you know where I am.

~ Psalm 139:1–3 (TLB)

Thank You, God, for making us who we are with the desires we have, the dreams and adventures we envision. Please help us to trust You as we wait for the good times ahead, knowing You love us and You smile when we are enjoying ourselves.

Chasing the White Cat

My beautiful yellow Lab hit the curb, hair furrowed in a ridge atop his back, like long grains of wheat in a field. He braced himself in a lunge position.

The white cat flew across the asphalt to the opposite sidewalk. Black pavement curved up from the small hill between Sammy and the white cat. It is a blind spot, where cars speed up the hill to a dangerous turn into our residential neighborhood where children and animals play. It is the reason our young neighbors moved.

"Sammy, stop!" The hair on *my* head started to rise.

Sammy's spine arched as he kicked off the sidewalk and then screeched to a halt hearing my command. His paws skidded to a stop. I ran up to him and grabbed his collar—his energy dissipated—he sulked, his eyes cast down.

"Don't you ever go out in that street. You remember Pepper? Pepper got killed out here!"

Our eyes met. How could we ever forget our Pepper, and that day? Sammy eyed me gingerly as I pointed to the black pavement street and then the white sidewalk, the beginning of our property. "Stay. Always stay!" He sat down obediently as I continued.

"No, never, no!" I waved my hands over the black

pavement street in front of my house like I could make it disappear. Sammy got it.

Leaning over, I wrapped my arms around his husky neck. Patting his head, I looked into his sad eyes searching mine for approval. "I always want to see Sammy play in the front for many years to come," I smiled. *He has always been my obedient one.*

Walking back to the house a thought persisted, God is like that with me. I really believe some days He has to yell at me to get my attention. All I see is the white cat.

How quickly I forget the past and it's lessons—just like Sam. Even if they've happened right in front of me.

I have learned to trust God's boundaries in my life, as Sammy has learned to trust mine. Even when I want that object of my attention so bad—I forget it can lead to danger. Thank God He's always watching and ready to warn me before I lunge in stupid spontaneity. And just as Sam can be enticed to run in so many directions down so many streets for endless reasons: squirrels, food, mail, cats, dogs, people—we too, each have a mixed bag of daily temptations to deny.

When I start off in the wrong direction, like heading to a clearance rack when I am already over budget, the Lord uses His shepherd's staff to restrain me. That divine hook from the sky has appeared many times and held me back from self-destruction. Later I come to my senses and realize I should have known better. But the Lord always loves me and hugs me again before I really even comprehend my mistakes.

Just as I hugged Sam, and he closed his eyes in my embrace of forgiveness and love, I'm reminded of the many times God has held me in blessed forgiveness and restored joy—something only a shepherd who really cares for his sheep would do.

What happiness for those whose guilt has been forgiven! What joys when sins are covered over! What relief for those who have confessed their sins and God has cleared their record. ~ Psalm 32:1–2 (TLB)

Thank You, dear Lord, for Your constant forgiveness. Grant me the grace to forgive my mistakes and bad choices when I forget to include You in every single part of my life. Thank You for straightening me out and warning me about *chasing cats*. Help me to listen and learn. Amen.

The Dynamic Duo

One day I visited a friend who had a four-month-old white Chihuahua decked with a striking pink collar that matched her gold-trimmed pink couch and leopard bed. Her collar assortment fascinated me. To name a few—white rhinestones, brass-studs on black, brown engraved leather, and blue sparkling sophisticate. And her wardrobe? Fur-trimmed jackets, brocade with buttons. Princess Di classic. Juicy Couture. Painted nails. She oozed *class*. This little doggie-diva makes a statement wherever she goes in her variety of designer dog-carrier totes.

My dogs have no clothing allowance. Sam is a field Lab—a free spirit—he sheds any article or fabric I try to attach to him, like the reindeer antlers at Christmas and his angel halo at Halloween. Benji wore one blue-striped sweater (no matching jeans) all winter to keep from shaking on the cold days. This past winter it was the same one everyday because I had misplaced the green one. He never complained. They eke *caz*, as in casual.

Benji is a purebred miniature schnauzer…and a born rebel. An outdated hippie, he prefers long nails, long hair and a scraggly beard (if I let him). He snaps when I trim the hair out of his eyes or ears, or cut his nails. It takes two to give him a puppy cut, one to hold him still as possible and the other to maneuver the scissors gingerly while he twists and turns to attempt a slippery escape.

My boys' fashion statements are pretty much limited to their collars. I try to match them with the same pattern until one loses his and then they are mismatched again. Recently, both have managed to dump their tags.

Today we headed to the neighborhood dog store, the parking lot buzzed with traffic and the lines were long. Benji stood alert in watch-tower position inside the cart's upper-level basket seat. Sammy navigated the aisles while I clung to his leash staccato-ing, "*Leave it*" commands as he nosed every bag lining the floor with an occasional quick grab. *Whap*, my cart hit a corner. *Bam*, Sammy's tail knocked the billboard. *Crash*. Down fell a sack of dog biscuits from the display.

"Look Mommy. Look at the big dog." The little boy grinned from the register queue pointing straight at Sam. By the time we arrived at the counter with our trusty rawhides, I almost forgot why we made this trip to the dog store.

"I need two ID tags. Both my dogs have lost theirs." The clerk pointed to the tag display on the counter. A bone, a heart, a circle, a black and yellow Batman. "Batman tags?" I asked excited. "Are they made of metal? I love Batman." The *Wham*, bash, crash TV text jumped to the forefront of my mind as quickly as it used to jump to the face of our television. *Suits Sam.*

"They are limited edition" the clerk added. "Yes, they are the same price."

Seconds later, the engraving machine spit out two new shiny metal tags. I attached each two-toned ID to the collars of my Big Batman and Little Robin. Sammy and Benji proudly bumped their way out the store in perfect character depiction and jumped into our Dogmobile.

We all have different personalities, likes and dislikes, and so do our dogs. The friend with the Chihuahua…is a ballerina. She likes fussing over her tiny girl and coordinating her wardrobe.

I grew up labeled "tomboy." Like mistress, like dog—I seldom dress up—preferring casual and comfortable. For years, I donned scrubs as work attire.

Today I'm thankful for these two designer tags at regular cost. For the opportunity of bringing my dogs into a store where they are welcome and amused. And now my masked-marauders stir happy reminders of a carefree childhood. A time when popcorn from the Revere-ware skillet was the evening treat and I sat on the lime vinyl couch with my brother's and our German shepherd, Prince. He lay on the family room floor as mesmerized by the television as we were.

Today I'm smiling at two gold and black tags dangling beneath matching collars and bright eyes. I'm reminded to be grateful for the little things. It's not what we look like or what we own—it's who we are that counts.

Sammy and Benji shine with one collar and one

special tag. Because they make strangers smile. They let children pet them…and the homeless. They are daily reminders to me that I have enough. That I must count my blessings and do good for others…just like Batman and Robin..

I am not saying this because I am in need, for I have learned to be content whatever the circumstances.
~ Philippians 4:11

Dear Lord, thank you for creating so many animal breeds, each with their innate personalities and behaviors. We are grateful for variety and the opportunity to choose dogs best suited to us. As they grow, help us to train them to become the best expression of themselves.

We are privileged to be expressions of your divine creativity—at our best when we appreciate simple things in life. The pleasurable moments with our loyal companions may be very different than the owner and the dog next door. And that's okay—for all of us!

Benji and Sammy donning their black ties for the processional at our wedding.

Lab without Borders

Everything about Sam, my yellow Lab, is limitless—the good and the bad.

He chases his tennis ball as if he were a Wimbledon contender, determined to use every joule of energy for every single return. His chest heaves and nostrils flare as he clenches the retrieved ball tight in his mouth unwilling to give up his prize, even for the next toss.

He will eat until he vomits, which he has done when I left food where he could get to it. Benji schnauzer will take a couple bites and leave his bowl all day. Of course it won't last long if I don't put it up, as Sam slyly inches over and inhales it like instant breakfast. He doesn't care how miffed Benji gets and how disapproving my rebuke.

Sam pushes my hand incessantly if he wants attention, no matter how much I shake him off. He gazes at me with rapt adoration—eyes ablaze with love—tail waving like a flag of celebration and mouth curved up in broad blessed joy. If I am inside, he wants inside. If I am outside, he wants outside. He doesn't understand *personal space*. It is not in his make-up.

He exhibits passionate feeling towards the people he loves, which are many. When visitors arrive,

Sam bounds with excitement to greet them, his body wobbling like that of a child on its first bike ride. If he is empty-mouthed, Sam will realize it before reaching them. He stops suddenly, turns around and surveys his field of view. A frantic search follows as he heads all directions to find a gift for his guest. It could be a toy, a sock, a piece of paper, a bone, a ball, a stuffed animal— anything—even one of my slippers.

He lies at, and frequently on, anyone's feet if they're seated on the couch. Often he tries to sit next to them by edging his rump up toward the sitting cushion since he is not allowed to climb up on the furniture. Whenever we are eating at the table, he follows us with puppy eyes and plops grunting on our feet if we ignore him. Sammy is in-the-moment, present and engaged. An emoter. Many friends have commented, "Sammy has great eye contact."

Sometimes I wish I were more like that with my Master, with God, whom I say that I love and serve with my whole heart. Then I would run with unhindered enthusiasm from start to finish with any project He gives me, loving God with all my heart, soul, mind and strength. Wherever God is and whatever He's up to is where I *want* to be. Wouldn't it be great if I were content to just sit at Jesus feet for long periods without care or concerned about how long I have been still?

Wouldn't it be amazing if I loved people as much as Sam and could eagerly share what I own without regard to age, sex, status, or intelligence—just because they are human beings made in the image of God? What is it that Sammy sees when he greets a person that makes him so excited?

Whatever it is, I want that quality. It reminds me of the heart of our Creator, of Sam's Creator.

I want to love without borders and greet others joyfully, uninhibited by my own self-conscious frailties, unmindful of how I look and what time it is, or distractions. Just drop everything—like Sam does.

Sam exemplifies what it looks like to love without borders. I watch Sammy and it's obvious—it's not about Sam. It's not about me. It's about sharing and interacting with others, realizing we all have something to give and receive from knowing each other. What a great way to live.

Jesus replied, " 'Love the Lord your God with all your heart, soul, and mind... Love your neighbor as much as you love yourself.' "

~ Matthew 22:37, 39 (TLB)

God, we marvel how much You love us to gift us with beauty all around us—the Milky Way and the North Star, the dainty dancing purple-and-yellow pansies, and the ladybugs on the grass blades. How did You instill a sense of ownership to pets just like You have given a farmer a sense of pride in his crops?

Each person has something to share of their worth, their gifts, their calling that is intrinsic to them, that our pets mirror of Your acceptance by granting us lavish love so easy.

Help us to love You like that every day no matter if the news be good or bad. There is so much more we need to know about You, God, and loving You, and the people You created around us. Give us desire, God, for more—the same kind of more that fuels Sam.

Instincts

"Benji, come on!" I waved my hands in the air, clasping a few choice nuggets. Benji remained at alert with one leg up and a stub pointing south, yapping at the two large dogs across the field. *If only I'd seen them earlier. Benji dances in the moment when other dogs are around.*

"Come on Benji!" I yelled a little louder, feeling a bit more tension as Sam my yellow Lab and I scurried far behind him. *Oh no!* My heart sank. Benji headed toward the yellow Lab who looked just like Sam, and the red Akita mix. *I've never felt comfortable about Akita's since I knew one who jumped on a little dog similar to Benji.*

Sam shot off from beside me, running toward Benji and the two rogues. *I hate dog fights.* My back tensed and heart raced anticipating trouble.

"No, Sam, come back!" Mercurial fear soared through my veins. Ever since my coworker's Lab was torn-up by two Rottweiler's, I fear big-dog duos.

Sam bounded at full speed. I stood helpless, too far away to make a difference no matter how fast I raced through the field. My dogs ignored my futile calls. Moving toward them, I noticed their owner springing from another direction. I held my breath as the dogs almost collided, then stopped and sniffed each other. Tense tails projected stiff as baseball bats. Sam's mane stuck straight up like a Mohawk, ruffled and ready. Benji, the wild card, stood erect dwarfed by three bellies above him.

The large yellow Lab broke the standoff by stepping back. He turned and jetted over to the mud puddle. Love those distractions!

The Akita now faced my defenders alone. She inched away and walked the other direction. Sam followed and proceeded toward the other yellow Lab and the fabulous mud pit.

Only Benji stood his ground where seconds before a testosterone war sizzled ready to erupt. I could see the face of the other owner now. Neither of us looked at each other. She sauntered expressionless toward her yellow Lab as he heaved his muddy torso onto all fours and shook, sloshing in his exquisite spa.

"Sammy, stay away from the mud!" I yelled two octaves higher—much relieved—but still hoping to escape the moment with as little damage as possible. Sam stopped his cadence just short of the mud pit—and about-faced toward me. Benji, still wearing the steely expression of a staunch German schnauzer, trotted victorious behind Sam.

I spun around heading back to my car like a chess queen zooming back to the protection of her side of the board. My now obedient pawns jumped into their section of the safety zone. Driving home, I realized, this queen did not have the best moves or instincts for her court at that moment.

I was glad Sam did not obey my first calls. If he had, Benji would have faced two big dogs alone, not realizing what a little hot dog he is to the others. After all, he has grown up daily looking at a 110–120 lb. Lab. In his mind he is a legend like the Babe, the big blue ox from Paul Bunyan stories.

Thank God, before Pepper, my other schnauzer died, he taught Sam courage to face other dogs. I still remember each time we entered the fenced doggie park at least four to six dogs would rush Sam at the gate. The gang would then press in on him as he dodged and ran to get away, unsuccessful with the more dominant ones who continued to tailgate him. That is, until he learned to stand up for himself and realized his true size.

I am so glad Sam followed his instincts and backed up Benji. He did not come back when I called him. As usual, when my reasoning is driven by fear, I do not make good decisions. It seems Sam knew Benji would not turn around and come—that he would try to stand up to the big dogs alone.

And Sam senses my fear. Didn't I tell a stranger at the drive-in yesterday Sam is my sensitive one— the one who is tuned into my emotions? I think Sam felt my fear for Benji. Although Benji causes Sam a lot of frustration, daily nipping his legs and ears, Sam tolerates him. And he looks out for his little brother.

God is the King who is teaching me how powerful those little pawns and some of their moves can be. I don't need to panic when I don't see the way out of a corner or a temporary checkmate in life. Sometimes the pawns can battle it out and the queen mothers in life just need to chill a little and let them face each other, with no losses.

PRAISE BE to the Lord, my Rock, who trains my hands for war, my fingers for battle. He is my loving God and my fortress, my stronghold and my deliverer, my shield, in whom I take refuge. ~ Psalm 144:1–2

Thank You, Lord, for creating circumstances in which I can't interfere. Cause me to trust You with situations beyond my control that may cause possible harm to those I love. May I leave my troubles in Your hands and not succumb to fear.

Help me trust You with my pets that they can respond with their God-given instincts to protect themselves with the bravado You have given them.

Observe, Observe, Observe

Woof, woof. Grrr. Woof.

I could hear Sam's barks from outside, while the house buzzed with estate sale customers. I ran my fingers over the smooth mahogany French provincial table top flipping the tags marked in four digits—then continued shuffling behind a man in a plaid shirt.

At the front door I stepped out to the porch and locked eyes with my concerned yellow Lab standing on the driveway. "I'll be right out Sam—be quiet." I placed my index finger to my lips and he stopped barking. Fastened to the trunk of the great valley oak, his double leashes were pulled taut. Benji, my miniature schnauzer, stood quietly by his side staring across the street, his leash draped on the ground.

Sammy just doesn't do well separated from me. Stepping back into the entrance, I scuttled through the rest of the house then rallied the dogs back to the car. By the time we returned home, Sam panted loudly.

The garage door whirred up. Benji jumped out first, but I grabbed his leash and held him back to let Sam jet to the water first. *Lap, lap, lap.*

Benji throated objections, peering intently at Sam's big head dominating the bowl. If I let Benji go, courteous

Sam would step back and wait until he was done.

"Benji, Sammy needs it more than you do," I cajoled my little one, curling my fingers tighter around his leash.

His irate black eyes locked on mine. He looked like a miniature horse tied to a post against his will.

Sam finished, lugged his head up, took a few steps and plopped on the garage floor to nap. Benji dipped his head in the bowl and lapped quietly. Then he ran to the side yard to squabble with the neighbor dogs.

So different. Sam's and Benji's needs—and how they express them—or not.

People can have difficulty expressing their needs too.

Recently I had a conversation with a disabled woman as we waited in line for a bathroom stall. Suddenly she said, "I wish people wouldn't always use the disabled stalls."

"Go ahead and go up first," I encouraged her noting her distressed tone.

"I have to go bad and I can't wait. So many times people use the stalls. I know they don't realize, but I have a hard time controlling myself."

"Just say something," I felt anxious for her.

"Oh, no—I could never do that."

"But the disabled stall was built for people that need it and you are that person."

She shook her head. "I don't want to make a scene."

Ever since that day, I only use the disability stall when no one else is around. It is better to use the smaller one in case a person arrives who needs the special accommodations.

Sammy is like that special-needs woman when it comes to his water capacity. Benji can wait longer to be hydrated because he is smaller and has a God-given advantage. Sam's needs are legitimate—just like the crippled woman in queue with the rest of us. With a personality like Sam, she will put herself last when it is her privilege to use the disabled stall. The majority of us, like Benji, tend to overlook the needs of the Sammy's surrounding us.

Maybe I needed this memory today. Just as Sammy needed water sooner than Benji, he also needed to know I was safe and close to him. Instead of disappearing into the estate sale and getting annoyed at his barking— maybe I needed to bring him home first so he wouldn't worry.

Sam communicates with barks and pants. As I learn to listen to Sam, maybe I can also learn to watch out a little more for shy people who are reluctant to share their genuine needs.

The wise in heart are called discerning, and pleasant words promote instruction. ~ Proverbs 16:21

Lord, help me to listen and look and feel the needs of others. Grant me more compassion so I am not so quick to judge or negate the actions that can annoy me when I am only looking out for myself.

Small Sticks

"I'm so afraid to get out there and share my product. It's so easy to stay at home and do the business stuff, but I have to move out now and face my fears," my friend voiced quietly. We stopped our walk at the edge of the lake and listened to the lapping of the water. I unleashed my dogs, Sammy and Benji, and we continued our discussion.

As novice entrepreneurs we were learning our new territory. Having exhausted our hot calls, we both lacked confidence and now faced unfamiliar territory—cold calls. The doors we needed to knock on were strangers or acquaintances. Our sensitive knuckles paused at the door of opportunity; we feared annoyed responses roaring, "Who is it?"

The confidence to sell our abilities seemed as unobtainable as the shore facing us from the other side of the lake.

"I hate doing it," she shook her head. "It is so hard. It's just not in me." She lifted a stick and sent it sailing through the air.

Sammy, ecstatic, shot off creating a wake from where he had been swimming in neutral, like a stalled jet ski that suddenly kicked into gear. We turned our attention to the dogs.

Benji's piercing cries hit the sky as he directed his gaze toward Sammy, who ignored him. The yipping of my little schnauzer retreating from the water's edge felt as useless as our elevator speeches.

Sammy glided hundreds of yards from the lake edge to retrieve his stick and Benji's bark reached a caustic level. The stick was far out of Benji's grasp and abilities, granting Sam the opportunity to practice what he was created for—swimming in deep water. If Sam couldn't locate the target stick, his immediate goal, he would stay out in the deep water until he grabbed something to bring back.

Sometimes he paddled around awhile, switching directions, never tiring, oblivious to my futile calls to return, he refused to return empty-mouthed. So, I threw another stick for him to retrieve or aimed a stone where the previous prize had landed.

The plopping sound helped Sam locate the floating stick and he started another victory lap home. He proudly gripped the symbol of his accomplishment well above the liquid surface inviting applause and prepared for his grand arrival and admiring fans. Benji's barks grew louder and his racing back and forth escalated exponentially with each yard Sam gained toward land.

"Good boy, Sam!" I called out clapping. "Great job."

It seemed Sam's enjoyment of our outing soared with each stick retrieval, unimpressed by the dampened spirit of his snarling little brother, bursting small snorts of frustration. As Golden Boy emerged from the water, his chest swelled with pride. His strong tail swept side to side as he flashed beautiful white teeth and courageous confidence. He knew he was a winner. Nothing could daunt his day, not even the small wet grayling, growling and gnawing at his legs. Sammy was on a roll—each return rewarded by my accolades and pats.

My friend entered Sam's world, enjoying the athleticism of a proven swimmer almost as good as Michael Phelps. She chucked a ball past the waterdog ballpark, over and over again, rustling Sam's head with approval each time he swiftly returned it.

Now, I focused on Benji. He looked dismal and small, even insignificant, when he was wet. In his lifetime he would never own the power stories Sam had accumulated: a puppy calendar dog, overcoming raging currents, pulling a loaded sled over fresh snowfall in frozen Sierra nights, competing in a mountain lake jumping contest.

While Sammy's ego was reinforced for success, Benji's little ego suffered defeat each time he had watched us pat Sam. He continued restlessly, shooting back and forth like a pinball stuck in an arcade machine, eying Sammy. I needed to distract him from looking at Sam. It only agitated him.

"Here Benji, here's a stick," I wriggled a small broken branch until Benji turned toward me. Damp curls dangled over his eyes.

"Benji, get the stick!" I threw the stick two feet from

shore. Benji hopped in and pounced on it, clamping down and wriggling it roughly in his mouth. He high-stepped back to shore and I grabbed it out of his mouth.

"Good boy, Benji. Great job."

I threw it again a couple feet further in the shallows, water no deeper than his belly. He raced to the stick, wrestled it in his mouth like a snake and carried it back in. "Great job, Benji. You are so good."

Benji tried to bite *his* stick from my hands but I threw it back in the water. The lake was quiet other than the occasional chirping of birds. My friend played ball with Sam and I challenged Benji slowly throwing his stick a bit further each time, but never beyond his ability to retrieve it.

When Sammy swam in from the water minutes later we prepared to leave. Benji ran over and hopped in front of Sam gripping his prize, exhibiting his accomplishment. Sammy ignored him. Benji didn't care. Now his mouth was full.

As we walked away it was clear; I needed to give up some of the unrealistic goals I had set for myself. I needed to quit looking at what others were doing and allow God to set my goals within reach of the calling and abilities he had given me. It was time to step out and get my feet wet and celebrate the small stick I brought back to Him, if that is what He wanted me to do. I would be content with who I am, too. Just like Benji.

We do not dare to classify or compare ourselves with some that commend themselves. When they measure themselves by themselves and compare themselves with themselves, they are not wise. We, however, will not boast beyond proper limits, but will confine our boasting to the field God has assigned to us.
~ 2 Corinthians 10:12–13

Dear God, thank You for knowing me so well that You give me tasks I can complete. Forgive me for times I have begrudged others because I am focused on their territory and have overlooked mine. Place me where You can use me and I can be content.

Help me to focus on Your hand and the daily tasks You place in front of me. Grant me a willing and energetic heart to take even the small steps of courage that will lead to accomplishment and success in Your eyes.

Me Too

Tonight Sam still limped on his big yellow paw. The first person I thought to call at this time of night was Sue, my doggie-loving tax lady.

"Hi Sue, I have a quick question other than the tax return. Sam has a red tender area and has been limping. He growls if I try to look at it."

"Do you have a muzzle?"

Benji peeked from around the corner.

"No."

"I'll come on over and bring one," she offered. "I need to get out of the house anyway."

While she drove I quickly changed out of pajamas into sweats, then ran into the garage and gathered an old comforter and towels for the kitchen floor. Sam likes padding to lie on.

Ding, dong.

Benji, alias "Squeaker," screeched, hitting notes octaves above a first soprano. My tension headache spiraled. Sam frantically searched for something to give Sue. He disappeared around the corner and barrelled back to the front door greeting her with a turquoise slipper and sweeping tail wags.

They followed her down the hallway to the family

room, where she looked at me and smiled while pulling out a leather cone-shaped muzzle.

"Watch this." Sue grabbed Sam by the collar and slipped the leather straps over his nose, fastening one behind his neck. He shook his head and pawed at the unwelcomed object attached to his snout.

It stayed in place at least five seconds and then dangled loosely, too short to clamp his mouth shut.

"I guess it's too small," she said studying the medium muzzle and sizing Sam's extra-large head. Sam clung near Sue unfettered as Benji quietly stood frowning in the distance.

Sue looked at me and winked, whipping out a leash. She quickly wrapped it around Sam's snout as if lassoing a calf in a rodeo. He squeezed his eyes and grunted, continuing to wag his tail as she led him into the kitchen where the comforter waited for our patient. Benji moved to the edge of the kitchen to monitor the newest event.

"Go on down, Sam," she coaxed as I gently angled him down into a side-lying position to examine his paw. She kept her hand tightly on the leash holding Sam's head as I began to check his pads. He pulled away at the sensitive ones.

"They are cracked," she noted as I rubbed them gently. No burns, just red. "Put olive oil on them."

"What about my aloe vera plant?" I hopped up and ran out into the light rain. Every summer when my nephew visits from Tennessee he cuts the pointed succulent leaves and splits each one carefully with a sharp serrated knife. Then he presses the moist liquid inside up against his face and neck sighing, "Ahhh." A smile seeped across my face just picturing Patrick's delight. Back in the kitchen I prepared the fresh leaf and bent down by Sue.

She braced Sam's paws as I pressed the succulent gently against his cracked pads. Fluid seeped into the dry crevices. Sam lay his strained head down on the floor and smiled.

Sue smiled too. "He loves it. Look at him. Let's just keep going. We'll do them all."

Benji stared from the kitchen door as Sam lay calm and closed his eyes. I repeated stroking the moist inner leaf on each paw.

"Okay Sam, We're done."

"Sam slowly raised himself up and moved into the family room, flopping onto the rug. Benji trotted into the kitchen and stood by Sue. I collected the leaves from the counter.

"Hi, little guy. Give me your paw?"

I turned around. Sue still sat on the pink comforter. Benji faced her, one front paw up in the air expectantly. In a second he circled in front of her and lay in Sammy's vacant place. Sue and I looked at each other amazed and chuckled. "I guess he's not afraid anymore. He saw Sam is okay."

Sue patted his head. "Looks like Benji wants the same treatment Sammy had."

I looked at him. He lay still, all four paws parallel to the floor without being coaxed or held. Wow.

There was nothing left to do but—so guess who had his paws done after Sam?

Sometimes we fear things until we see someone else go before us.

Sometimes we watch people enter relationships, afraid we could never be in one, until a friend succeeds and finds happiness. Or we watch a friend use a Nook or GPS and decide we might try a step forward even though we are tech challenged. Or we taste our neighbor's home grown tomatoes and decide a garden may be worth the work.

It could be a decision to switch jobs or houses, after someone close to us discovers fulfillment despite the work and pain of transitioning. Their courage gives us courage to move forward into something we have been thinking about.

How many times have we stood at a distance— learning from others—afraid to try ourselves? We need to follow suit, like Benji. Trying something new just takes the first step forward and trusting in the Mighty hands that care.

In God I trust; I will not be afraid. What can man do to me? ~ Psalm 56:11

Lord, thank You for the many opportunities that surround us daily. Help us to step out in faith when we feel like we are missing out, watching others get the good stuff. Grant us trust and courage to move toward something new. We open ourselves to receive all You have for us.

Leashes

"Sammy, that's enough—it's time for the leash." I whirled Sam's leash in the air and called to get his attention, carefully stepping on clumps of grass in the muddy field. Benji and I bee-lined toward the light rail tracks—the direction Sammy's delighted, excited Labrador nostrils were leading him.

Initially, we left the car in this urban area and headed to an abandoned parking lot for doggercise. Cyclone fences provided boundaries so Sam and Benji could run free. But the sight of a beat-up, unpainted car, chipped lettering on the buildings and outdoor merchandise protected by guard dogs, altered our course.

I tugged Benji's leash reminding him to follow me as he strained his head in the opposite direction—inches from a tossed and tantalizing fast-food wrapper. Thankful Benji had his leash on, I scurried toward Sam feeling uneasy. He rushed from one spot to another traversing the unkempt lot in full dog throttle between the commuter train and the car-lined street where we had parked. Maybe this wasn't the best way to kill time between my appointments.

Now, true to form, Sam exercised restraint and beckoned to my call even though his head faced the tracks and his eyes longingly scanned them. I clipped on his leash, breathing a sigh of relief, and patted his head. "Good boy, Sam. I shouldn't have freed you in this field. There are too many fascinating new smells, I don't know the area and there are no fences." Usually I choose fields with boundaries around them.

Walking back to the car, I thought about the call from a friend this morning. She confessed a sudden surge of sin and temptation had surfaced once more in her life. Just as the scent of that old hamburger wrapper drew Benji, she struggled with an addiction she had nurtured years without restraint—until she asked God into her life. Then, she submitted to the Lordship of Christ, and allowed Him to lead her as the Master of her soul. She found freedom from the pull of devouring garbage that left her feeling sick to her stomach, at odds with herself, her Master, and the good life she had so carefully built.

"I know what to do," she told me. We recently repeated this talk. She was starting a pattern, parking in her abandoned past. Like me and the dogs, she was romping around in a minefield of tantalizing scents. Even though I didn't understand the attraction or the pleasure of a trashed old field, I felt my dogs strain against my pull in the right direction and the intensity of their desire. I understood the safety of a leash.

I reasoned with my friend. "You have the potential to destroy everything you have worked so hard to build— your whole life is at stake." We talked. We prayed. It wasn't enough. She needed a leash.

I told her I would call her boss if she didn't call him herself in twenty-four hours—even if she hated me for it. Just like I love my dogs, I love my friend the way God loves me. And God uses leashes—I've got one too. But I don't need mine for this muddy old field—I've got another field.

And so the leash snapped back on. She made the call. I felt relieved and hopeful that she is backing out of the quagmire, willing or not. The leash from heaven guided by a compassionate and wise Master is tugging her now, away from train-wreck territory.

Leashes restrict. They restrain us from running wild. But they also keep us close to our master. They provide limits and security as we trust in His love and goodness to protect us. Especially when we aren't looking for headlights or listening for a whistle.

So I say, live by the Spirit, and you will not gratify the desires of the sinful nature. For the sinful nature desires what is contrary to the Spirit, and the Spirit what is contrary to the sinful nature. They are in conflict with each other, so that you do not do what you want. But if you are led by the Spirit, you are not under the law. ~ Galatians 5:16–18

Dear God, help me to walk with You today and serve You today. Help me to trust You to meet my needs in Your time and Your ways. Guard me and guide me to follow You for the purposes You have for me. Lead me away from temptations that beckon my weak will, and protect me from forces around me that would plunge me into despair.

I trust in Your love for me. I lean on Your wisdom and strength. I will take drastic measures against destructive desires that have the capacity to lead me away from Your green pastures. I receive Your courage and strength and honor You by my obedience and trust. I will follow You today, Lord, one step at a time. Rein me in and reign in me.

The Rooster and the Beast

"Jon, I am so mad at Benji!" I vented to my friend as we walked our dogs along the river.

"You can't blame a dog for following his nature," he chided. "Sometimes we forget that even though they're domesticated, they are still animals." They revert to what their true nature is in certain situations. In Benji's case—he was hunting."

Earlier, before we crossed the footbridge, I had parked near a historic town tucked in the county suburbs where roosters roam like they are home on the range. They hang out at the drive-in, at the park, and one or two can be seen ambling up the road at any given time.

I scouted the sloping streets for other people or dogs near the footbridge. All clear. "Okay, Benji." I un-clicked his leash glad to give my little guy the freedom his big brother, a fairly obedient Labrador retriever, experiences routinely. "Follow Sam," I coaxed Benji who stood motionless while I eyed Sam sniff unseen shrub deposits, his pink nose flaming.

What I didn't see was the rooster.

Instead of clipping along at Sam's heels, Benji shot off in the opposite direction like a startled jack rabbit. But he was not the prey—he was the predator.

My silver-gray rabbit-like Benji, bounded across the street and up the hill. I glimpsed the back of his cropped woolly tail bobbing behind the flapping wingspan of a white, red-bearded rooster. Feathers flew as the rooster squawked and rocked up the street as fast as his claws could pedal the pavement. My voice seemed to fade in the breeze behind them as they skittered up the road and out of sight. *I'll never see him again*—I panicked.

Thank God the rooster decided to turn around.

"Benji! Benji!" They reappeared from the top of the hill. The rooster had slowed and seemed to be limping. Benji's snout glued to the crower's behind as if wearing a feathered crest. I ran toward him, scolding the wind. For a moment he looked up and then past me, fixing his pupils on a spot across the street. Two brown roosters peeked out between the blades of tall grass.

"No!"

Too late. He bee-lined just beyond my grasp. Now he purged the street of his newest prey—about-face toward one pitiful loner who took off flying—straight into a cyclone fence.

The fence shook with the force of his chest. I was livid. Benji, wide-eyed and perky-eared, ignored my ghastly presence. Now I wanted the blood of a German schnauzer as much as he wanted the blood of that rooster. Praying for a miracle, I got it. Just as he lunged across the ditch to *terrier-ize* the next victim, I grabbed his torso and flipped him on his back. Kneeling squarely above Benji, he avoided my eyes and squirmed like a stuck pig. Suddenly he was still—and gazed back in silent innocence.

Fresh from the scene, I described it now to my dog-walk friend, greatly disappointed in Benji's lack of compassion, Jon stopped me. He held my gaze. "You can't blame animals for following their intrinsic nature. They're still animals."

"I had the same thing happen with my girl this week." He shared the antics of his mellow standard pink poodle. "It really surprised me. Rudy took off and got hold of a duck. She's never done that before. She had it in her mouth and refused to let go." He grimaced. "I never thought my girl would hurt anything, but she had that duck in her mouth. It was a reminder she's first an animal with an animal nature. I can't get mad at her for following her instincts." He paused, "I'm just going to have to be more vigilant."

My anger toward Benji drained like water down a kitchen sink—washed down by reason. Schnauzers historically hunted rats and foxes. I can't blame his behavior toward critters any more than I can be upset with Sammy, my water dog, who can't stay out of water even if it's in the form of mud.

It made me think how people are in similar situations.

How can I judge my friends possessed with consuming passions? Some adrenaline-junkies run after every adventure they can find, always ready to relay their latest discovery. Their dreams culminate at peaks of mountains. Some want only to conquer the latest apex of technology. If I try to connect when they are in their zone, whether checking on their newest tool, fishing rod, or All-Star, they cannot see or hear me. They are a million miles away—just like Benji.

Tonight, I was supposed to go out with a friend who changed our plans at the last minute. Nothing new. It happens when she meets a man. It is her nature to focus on finding a companion like he is a moving target. I cannot judge her. She is doing what she always does. So I will do what I like to do and write and hang with my boys.

Then later I'm going on a funny-movie hunt and if the phone rings, I can't talk. We will be in our own little world of imagination—the little beast, the big beast and the beauty.

Therefore judge nothing before the appointed time; wait till the Lord comes. He will bring to light what is hidden in darkness and will expose the motives of men's hearts. At that time each will receive his praise from God. ~ 1 Corinthians 4:5

Lord, thank You for the dogs You gave me, who were bred for inherent purposes I am slow to comprehend. And thank You for friends as diverse as the different breeds of animals. In all their God-given interests, fascinations and pursuits lead them to balance and moderation, so they run with grace and dignity, not in crazy obsession like Benji. Help my friend to accept herself, a natural beauty, and bring her a mate who will hunt her down just like Benji chased that irresistible rooster—driven by an inbred animal instinct You placed in him.

There Are Other Dogs, Too

Rrrrr. Yip. Yap. RRrrr.
WOOF. Woof. MMmmm.
RRRrrrrr. Yap, yap, yap, yip …
Woof, woof. Woof, woof, woof …

The ruckus from the living room transported me out of my chair to check the cause of the commotion. *Someone is out front*, I figured. Sure enough, Benji stood on all fours on his watch chair at the window. His ears flipped out with each bob of his agitated head, while his barks whirred like a dishwasher in full wash mode.

Sammy stood at the other end of the window. His hair bristled down his back forming a ridge like a Mohawk on a porcupine. Sam's emotional Richter scale passed 7.0, his back legs pumping up and down so hard his rump revved off the ground every couple seconds shaking the coffee table.

"What is it?" I headed toward the living room window—the boys observatory. Outside, a strange woman stood with two leashed dogs, a yellow Lab and a golden retriever—allowing both to sniff the ragged edges of our front lawn.

"You're not the only guys around here that can

smell other people's lawns." I frowned. "There are other dogs, too."

They ignored me and continued the ruckus. Benji's yips melted into whimpers as soon as the unwelcome visitors disappeared from view. Then he jumped off his chair and ran around to the front door. The house abruptly settled to a normal decibel level and I returned to my office.

My thoughts reverted to my activities prior to the interruption. I had just left an apology on a colleague's voicemail. How I resisted following through on this, even though I knew it was the right thing to do. Although I also felt offended by the other person—God had nudged me to own my issues in our falling-out.

Words I just spoke to Benji and Sammy ricocheted back to me. *You're not the only dogs, there are other dogs too.* Why was it so hard to admit my part in the argument? Regardless if I was right or wrong—my delivery was the usual, escalating rant no different than my boys' over-the-top reaction.

Offending others and being offended are part of life and growth. We teach our children how to give and receive an apology to prepare them for adulthood. We learn constructive criticism is helpful and necessary, whether from God or man.

Last week a friend confided in me after her husband unintentionally hurt her feelings. "God is teaching me when I am offended, I must overcome evil with good. I can never overcome evil with evil." It's automatic to pay back a wrong with a wrong—instead of a right. The latter we have to think about, pray about and practice with God's help.

I wince at words to ponder spoken through wise counselors. "You're not perfect either." "Stop the judgment. Look at the resistance," meaning the part that wants to defend me more than consider the other person's point of view and give them the benefit of the doubt.

I have entitlement issues in my life, just like my fidos. In the same way I admonished them, God has rebuked me through others, for a positive end. How much am I willing to listen? As much as Benji when his wails turn to whimpers, caught up in his feelings—and his feelings only?

I can't expect my dogs to understand perspective. They are limited in their understanding. But God can expect me to admit my faults and live up to His expectations. He made me in His image with unlimited access to His patience and wisdom, forgiveness and correction. And He gave me a world view that extends beyond my skin, my lawn and my life. It's not all about me. Just ask Sammy and Benji. They are learning, too.

"Come to me, all you who are weary and burdened, and I will give you rest. Take my yoke upon you and learn from me, for I am gentle and humble in heart, and you will find rest for your souls. For my yoke is easy and my burden is light." ~ Matthew 11:28–30

Lord forgive me for justifications I use to continue bad behavior and cling to selfishness. I am deeply aware of my feelings and how others affect me, and so often unaware of how I affect others.

You have placed all wisdom at my disposal to learn and grow through praying to You, listening to You and loving You, my Wonderful Counselor and humble Master who is gentle and willing to teach even distracted, stubborn humans like me.

Enchanting Ears

"He's so cute! He looks like a little stuffed bear—and what cute ears!" The woman tousled Benji's head as we waited for my friend in the bistro foyer for a late lunch.

When she arrived, we found a shady spot on the veranda. Before we sat down, I tied Benji's leash to the metal chair frame. The waiter stepped through the door to the patio area and greeted us.

"Oh, look at those cute ears!" The waiter's blue eyes danced with love at first sight.

"What's his name?" He placed menus before us and bent down on one knee to court my reluctant salt-and-pepper schnauzer.

Too bad Sammy isn't here, I thought, *to make up for his brother's lacking social graces*. Of course, Sammy doesn't have small ears that stick up and bend like Benji's, and that seems to be what enamors his admirers.

"Come here Benji." The waiter extended his arm and rubbed his thumb and forefinger together in circles. "He's got the kind of ears you just want to pinch." He was as fixated on petting Benji's ears at the moment, as I was on the menu propped before me.

My eyes fastened on the prawn tacos with all the

delicious trimmings. I was ready right now. "Benji, let him pet you," I urged with no authority. Benji backed into reverse and sat down at alert underneath my chair.

"He's like this with anyone new," I apologized. "If my other dog were here you would be greeted with gusto."

"Oh well, you'll get used to me before you leave." The waiter stood up, smiling down at Benji's signature frown, and turned to take our order. When he left, he stole another glance at Benji, still hiding from strangers and the summer sun.

Minutes passed, and our waiter was back. He set down two beautiful glasses of water, each half filled with ice and a sliver of lemon. Then he planted a little blue plastic bowl of water in front of Benji. Benji didn't budge.

"You'll warm up to me, little fellow," he said in passing.

When our tacos and seafood salad came we gushed, happy to receive the blessings of a wonderful meal. It was everything we expected. We passed the time talking and catching up. Every time the waiter came back he'd check on Benji and try to coax him out from underneath the chair. Not until we were leaving the courtyard, did the waiter have a chance to give Benji a little pat on his back.

"Come back again and next time you'll warm up to me." Benji stood close to my legs, his face remained expressionless as we walked off to the enduring compliment, "Oh those ears."

For whatever reason, the waiter and the woman—really took to Benji's ears.

Truth is stranger than fiction. Sometimes there are innocuous physical characteristics that draw us to each other—innate and undeniable. The kind of reasons that spur philosophical quotes like, "The heart has reasons that the reason does not know."

In nursing school, a conversation with a classmate stayed with me for years.

"I hate my hands," she said curling her fingers underneath her palms. "They're like chubby little stubbies." She laughed. "But do you know my husband loves them? He thinks they are adorable. It's one of his favorite things about me." She paused smiling a secret smile.

"And he hates his nose," she laughed. "It's crooked and he thinks it is way too big for his face. But I love his nose!" she blurted emphatically. "I think it's cute and would never want him to change it. He doesn't understand that."

We exited the restaurant today—Benji bearing his social frown. It seems he will never understand just how cute his ears are to admirers.

I praise you because I am fearfully and wonderfully made; your works are wonderful, I know that full well. My frame was not hidden from you when I was made in the secret place. When I was woven together in the depths of the earth, your eyes saw my unformed body.

~ Psalm 139:14–16

Dear Lord, thank You for creating each of us with such an amazing variety of noses and mouths, fingers and toes, eyes and even ears that we cannot doubt You wanted to make all of us different and varied and wonderful—on purpose.

Thank You for people who love us just as we are. And thank You that we love our dogs with a pug nose or long snout, short legs or long, with or without a tail, shaggy or hairless and even floppy or clipped ears! We honor Your creativity in our dogs and in ourselves, the people made in Your image. Amen.

The Trouble with Coyotes

"I cried from the car all the way down into town," my friend Cathy said quietly after our writing class. Her face flushed depicting the emotion she felt after discovering her dogs were missing earlier this evening. "I looked up from the living room and noticed they weren't there. When I opened the sliding glass door and they didn't come—that's when I saw the unlatched gate. But God was with me from the time I started searching." She swiped a moist eye and smiled.

"It started as soon as I jumped in the car and began heading toward town. Everyone I asked along the way had seen them just before I got there. It was like God was paving the trail." She sighed. "But when I realized they had crossed the bridge out of town, I was worried. Thank God they were just on the other side. There were coyotes and it was getting dark."

Coyotes. They had triggered a recent scare with Sammy, my yellow Lab.

"I had Sam at my Dad's in the country one night and let him out around ten o'clock. When he didn't come back right away, I started worrying."

"Sam. Sam!" My voice disappeared in black air.

"I hope the coyotes don't get him," Dad piped up.

"What? He's so big!" I answered, alarmed.

"It doesn't matter. One will woo a dog away to play and then the pack jumps on them."

"Exactly, that's what they do." Cathy frowned. "I was worried about Daisy—she loves to play with other dogs. I'm so happy my dogs are home," she crooned, preparing to drive back home.

Later I spoke with my nephew by phone and reviewed our conversation about dogs and coyotes. "It's not much different than people," he surmised.

"You mean coyotes wooing people?" I asked.

"No, I mean people and people. One guy will say, "Let's go fight outside and then when he gets the guy out there, all his other friends jump on him."

"That's terrible. That's right. I remember you had a fight last year in a pub at Lake Tahoe."

"Yeah, I've been in a few fights. That one was ten to four. They don't fight the way they used to. It's not the right way. They use to fight with, with…"

"You mean fighting fair?" I asked.

"Yeah. They pull out knives and weapons and gang up. It's not the way it was in the old days—they are brave in a group, but they can't go it alone."

That night at my dad's, I sighed with relief when Sam finally emerged from the black hole and appeared at the front door. Who knows what happened down there by the road?

But what about us?

We may work in jobs where some people have two faces. They woo us as friends when we are alone, but in their clique they gossip or backbite. They have a double standard. Within their clique they cover each other for unethical behavior like shopping on the internet or late lunches and breaks. Yet they gang up on individuals outside their circle, quick to report any perceived discrepancies and target them for trouble.

Even if we are frightened we are not alone in these situations. Joshua is a biblical example of a responsible man who, though fearful, moves forward into unknown enemy territory. "Be strong and very courageous," God told him time and again.

We display courage when we do what is right using truth as a weapon to defend ourselves and others or as a light to guide us. When we are doing the best we can and trusting God, He will pull us through any situation or trial. We can be confident God is with us and He will support and protect us. He has our back no matter who opposes us.

He can provide unusual means of help like the strangers guiding Cathy to her dogs, or He can give us supernatural courage to defend ourselves as Sammy may have displayed that dark night. In the end, His light will shine in the darkness of our circumstances and we will be saved from our enemies.

Have I not commanded you? Be strong and courageous. Do not be terrified; do not be discouraged, for the Lord your God will be with you wherever you go.
~ Joshua 1:9

Lord, thank You for the small steps and large leaps You provide to intervene and care for our animals in ways we may not even fathom. Help us realize You can provide inner strength and alter circumstances in our behalf when we are surrounded by enemies until we are safely home.

Oasis around the Bend

"See? Those are my dogs." I pointed to my Toyota dogmobile parked outside the acupuncturist's office. Sammy panted from the back seat and stared at us, wide-eyed. Benji stood in the driver seat looking the opposite direction—focused on something across the street.

"They are smart?" Dr. Lee's Chinese accent rose.

"Very smart." I read Sammy's eyes—and suddenly felt anxious, painfully aware Sammy looked hot and thirsty. "That's why they train Labrador Retrievers for guide dogs. Sammy is my smart one and Benji is my stubborn one." I turned from the window and grabbed my purse.

"Thank you for showing me your dogs." Dr. Lee sounded sincere and glad to see them as I rushed past him—but not half as glad as the boys were to see me when I opened the car door. Today's heat signaled the turn of seasons—spring had ended. Time to change our car routine.

"Sorry guys," I said, pouring the rest of my water bottle into their emptied plastic Tupperware and replacing it on the console. Their heads touched mine as their tongues lapped rapidly.

How can I reward my boys for being so good and patiently waiting?

Recalling a nearby park, I drove around the corner. Planted in the middle of a suburb lay a park with a rolling green lawn and heritage trees—like an oasis in the middle of the desert—devoid of dogs or people. Sammy and Benji hopped out of the hot car and flew by me like Frisbees onto the shaded lawn.

Moments ago they had no idea how their lives would change by a quick drive around the corner.

A quick jaunt around a bend brought delight and avoided disaster.

Moses led the Israelites through the Red Sea, a huge barrier between freedom and their Promised Land, only to find the next destination a hot dry desert called Marah. Only a small pool of bitter water to share among a million, the people grumbled at Moses and God. Moses prayed and, at God's instruction, he threw a stick of wood in the water suddenly turning it sweet. The people drank. Amazingly, just around the corner (Genesis 15:27) God led them to Elim—a place where there were twelve springs and seventy palm trees!

I watched my Big and Little frolick joyfully in their modern-day Elim after a hot and bitter wait in their own Marah minutes ago. I bet from their doggy viewpoint... it felt like the heat would never end.

It feels like I have been wandering around in a desert myself lately. Especially this past week, feeling stuck and dry in my career change where every door slammed shut—before I even reached the welcome mat.

What is going on, God?

So this morning I spoke to a dear friend, another budding entrepreneur. She's so new to the realm of entrepreneurship she couldn't pronounce the word! But after we prayed together, for each other's ideas, gifts and calling, I felt something open up—something called possibility. Instead of stupidly staring down the closed doors, she pointed out the windows I have ignored. She described how fun it is to climb through those open windows because she already did.

"I've been chasing rainbows again, looking up and down the streets for a key to fit the door,"

"Why?" Her eyebrows raised. "What's the problem with climbing through the window?"

"I don't want to get in that way. It .doesn't feel legit…like I'm breaking in."

Reason came later. I'm not breaking windows. I'm not destroying anything, except valid options. I'm just embarrassed   others will see I'm climbing a window instead of opening the door with a key that's been given to me. So here is my test.

I either grumble like the children of Israel and drink the last drops of an empty water bottle or I climb in through the window and turn on the tap inside the house where my dream convenes. So today I decided, it's time to stop waiting and knocking on doors. I need to move toward a window. Of course, I will need to exercise courage, but that's next. Right now, I'm heading that direction.

I can almost hear my stepdad's jovial voice prompting me from his heavenly oasis and divine perspective, "it's just around the bend." The same way I reassured Sammy and Benji moments ago.

Where there is no vision the people perish.
~ Proverbs 29:18 (KJV)

Lord you have seen my struggle and my pride. I want to walk through a door that is not open. Help me if I'm resisting other options. Assure me again you will provide in these dry times as I allow you to guide me in unfamiliar paths.

Grant me patience to stay put and trust your sense of direction. Show me the hidden places and open spaces ahead. When the time comes, help me know I can jump through a window if the door is stuck. Prod me when to go. Free me from the confines of conformity and transform my thoughts with faith that trusts beyond what is visible.

That Thing You Do

"I'm impressed with your calmness," my friend stated from the kitchen taking another bite of his sandwich. His pink standard poodle, Ruby, sat quietly by his legs.

Benji and Sammy circled by the door, Sam's tail like a soft scythe in the dormant air of the entry hall. Benji jumped up on his back legs hopping in a vertical skip to the door. *Woof, woof. Yap, yap. Woof. Yap. Yipe, yipe.*

I ran to answer the door. Halfway there, I turned around and gave Jon a puzzled look. The bell rang again, the cacophony re-ignited.

"What?" I yelled over the ruckus.

"That noise." He stood in the hall contorting his face, twenty feet from the door. He lifted his hand as if to break the waves of sound, and clutched his ears.

"What noise?"

"That high-pitched noise." He wrinkled his nose. "The high yipe. It would drive me crazy."

"Oh, *that*!" I shrugged my shoulders, thinking he's the second man to remark about Benji's expressive watchdog antics recently.

"Benji never barked until two months ago," I mused once again. "He's always been so quiet I almost worried. Now at eighteen months old he suddenly found his voice."

Jon grimaced.

I grinned, relieved that Benji could bark. "It's similar to how a mom feels when her toddler hasn't spoken a word by two. My nephew, Chris, didn't put any words together until he was three. Now that Benji found his voice—he's using it constantly."

Isn't that so like us? We don't know we can write, sing, play guitar, use a mouse, take a beautiful photo, fix a car, hit a ball, or paint a mural. Then, when we find a hidden talent, we are relentless, experimenting with our now obvious gift.

I once had a neighbor who discovered a passion—bricklaying. He started with a row of bricks to line his flower garden. Then he constructed a brick mailbox, retainer walls, and a brick path to the door. Every time I walked Hannah past his house, sure enough, he'd built another brick project over the weekend. I always wanted to see his backyard and secretly wondered at his wife's response. Whatever and however, he had found his bricks!

I think God smiles, even grins down from Heaven upon all of us, His creation, and his little mini-creators. A chip off the Cornerstone, the Eternal Rock. He doesn't mind how good we are or how doggone annoying to others around us. He's just glad we're learning to express ourselves.

Some of us are late bloomers. We find our hidden natural talents later than others. Chris became so verbally intuitive, he went on to cut a rap CD at sixteen years old. And who knows what ethereal pitch Benji will be able to accomplish in another ten years. Wait until Jon comes over for lunch then!

For we are God's workmanship, created in Christ Jesus to do good works, which God prepared in advance for us to do. ~ Ephesians 2:10

Dear Lord, thank You for loving us and creating us with inherent expressions, uniquely ours. The sound of our voice, the way we walk, our pace, movements, and interests. All are a part of the wonderful variety and creation You inspired.

Thank You for matching us with our animals. You knew that Benji's yipe would not bother my ears, and that Sammy's larger than life torso and tail would make me laugh. You knew Ruby's calming presence would bless Jon and bring him peace. Thank You, Lord, for handpicking our pets, knowing us and knowing them!

No to the Nose

Frustrated, I tossed the leash, the towel, the gloves and the empty vinegar bottle in the trash. It was ten o'clock at night and Sam was rolling on the grass on our little berm in front of the house—after his vinegar bath.

"You're not coming in the house tonight, Sam, I'm really not happy about this."

Fifteen minutes earlier we were headed home from an evening walk. Stars shone and cool air provided welcome relief from a hot summer day. Suddenly Sam and Benji thrust their noses into our neighbor's hedge. Even in the dark I could see the leaves shake and hear the rustle of a critter.

"No! Heel! Leave it!"

It was too late.

Sammy's body quivered in anticipation, and the hair on his back bristled as he lunged along the hedge, intent on getting the hidden creature of the night.

I held Benji back but had to let go of Sam's leash as he lunged forward, catapulted by his powerful hind legs. The cat darted from the bushes toward the house, then suddenly turned and stopped.

Sam stood barking at full throttle. The creature hissed, challenging him. *Don't hurt it, Sam*, I prayed as Benji and I stood on the sidewalk. We observed a flat, white tail stiff and straight like a tiny lodge pole pine.

Wow, that's an odd cat. It remained motionless, it's tail fixed. Sam faced it and stopped barking. He shook his head briskly and turned trotting quickly toward me and Benji his eyes lowered. I leaned over to grab his leash and inhaled. My nose confirmed the cat—was a skunk. As Sammy panted, each putrid breath registered high on the skunkalizor.

"Sam, you really did it this time! See what a mess you caused by disobeying me? How are we going to get that pungent spray out of your mouth?" Sammy's eyelids dropped a notch.

Disobedience has a price—not only for us, but for others around us. Sometimes we can't just fix the problems caused by our lack of self-control. We know from prior history to listen to the voice of our Master. Still we lunge into shopping splurges. Pleasure-hunt catastrophes begin by fascination or curiosity, and ultimately fights with demons in the dark that can plague us for days to come.

Unfortunately, I did let Sammy in to sleep that night because he kept whimpering. The next morning my bedspread had a hint of essence of the wild. I tried tomato juice since Sam's vinegar bath failed to remove the smell-effects.

I'm hoping Sam has learned from this. When I say no to indulging his big pink nose—he can trust me. My favorite part of Sam is his nose—but it's also the part that can get him in a lot of trouble.

"I love you, Sam," I said, kissing the top of my Lab's golden head, despite the skunk aroma.

Sam is no different than me. I know God kisses my head every night when I finally settle to sleep no matter how much trouble I've gotten myself into. I disobey his commands daily in tangible ways or even intangible—like worrying about things—things I cannot control.

I washed Sam again just like God in His love washes my soul daily. He cleanses me of the effects of activities of the mind, soul, and body that bring the smell of the world and death instead of the fragrance of His life and peace. Fragrance that springs from within to all those who follow His leading, heeding the restraint He provides through the Holy Spirit. As we listen to His voice. And walk close to Him. And trust His "yes" or His "no" in the daylight hours and the dark moments.

If only you had paid attention to my commands, your peace would have been like a river, your righteousness like the waves of the sea. ~ Isaiah 48:18

Thank You, Lord, that You know my nature. *The spirit is willing but the flesh is weak.* You understand my spontaneous blunders and short-sighted misinterpretations. Wash my soul in forgiveness when I make poor judgments and fail to listen to Your voice robbing myself and others of peace. Keep me humble so I stop to listen and look for Your truer, larger perspective before I create avoidable crisis.

Help me to forgive myself even while bearing the consequences of foolish rash actions. Keep me from the trap of "if only" and realize there will always be a "next time." Thank You for Your love and commitment to teach me. I want to learn my lessons so when next time comes You and I will both know that I have grown and gained wisdom from past mistakes.

Hidden Treasures

"Four dollars a basket? That's way too much! I can get blackberries free off the bushes at the park!" I popped one of the dozen tart berries into my mouth. "And these aren't even as sweet!"

Last night we stopped at a store on a drive through the hills of California gold-rush country. But gold is hard to find these days and money doesn't grow on trees, so the dog-awful price for a dozen berries really bothered me. *I'll pick some tomorrow*, thanks to Sam.

He has really helped my pocketbook this past two weeks by leading us to two outdoor markets—*hidden treasures*. Today we ventured to the first one.

"Sammy, come on," fifty yards away Security Guard Sam lay looking over the soccer field near the truck where a man sat alone in his cab. Benji, leashed as usual, stuck as close to me as chewed gum while we edged our way through brambly shrubs that fringed the park perimeter. I poked through thousands of thorny branches laden with blackberries, many already past prime from the hundred-degree temperatures. That's when we eyed the hidden jewels, dangling, one or two, ripe-n-ready among bundles of dried clumps.

Uumm, uumm. Benji whined. I lifted branches and peered into the underworld of twigs and thorns. I wasn't leaving until the box had enough jewels to crown a pie!

We made our way up one side of the park. Benji ignored the berries and sniffed the green grass, while I picked non-stop, avoiding the prickles that cut through my stained latex gloves.

Sam eyed us occasionally, rising to match our stride each time we moved a few links along the fence line. He settled down at a distance. *Wasn't he pleased to see me so happy with his find?* I had never seen the bushes, only occasionally visiting this park so Sam could retrieve with *Chuck-it*. One day Sam stopped chasing the ball and ran to investigate behind the bushes. My initial displeasure at Sam's disobedience transformed to childish delight when we discovered a quarter of a mile of my favorite berry bushes!

It seemed Sam relished his dog sentry role as much as I enjoyed picking blackberries. When we returned home the dogs jumped out of the car. Sam ran to the water bowl. I greeted my nephew and his friends elated—"Try some fresh berries!"

"Sweet!" they chimed. We all rejoiced in the comfort of homemade pie.

One previous Saturday, a few weekends before the morning sun dominated our suburb streets, Sam veered off our beaten dog walk path.

"Okay Sam, you're bored with the same old route," I chuckled as I let him lead us into a new neighborhood … Benji and I followed.

Multiple blocks later, we passed a family's garage sale. Nothing seemed interesting at first—so we kept going. But on our return trip we stopped, to the delight of the children. I secured Sammy and Benji to a gate under shade trees. Instantly, a throng of mini-admirers gathered round them oohing and ahhing. I left them to browse.

"Mom, I wish I could wear your clothes," a lady addressed a sophisticated, middle-aged woman who had joined her daughter. I took the cue and sauntered over to the clothes hung on a line strung across the top of the garage, and chose the black leather jacket.

"How does it look?" I asked a young mom, glancing at the dogs as two children stooped down to place a bowl of water before the Two Princes of Doggieland.

"Fits you perfect!" she exclaimed. "Try the other ones."

We left with a little pile of hidden treasures and a promise to come back soon with the money and the car. Suddenly, I had my fall wardrobe!

Again, Sam, my adventurous field Lab led us to *hidden treasures* because he chose a different route than the shorter familiar that completes my to-do list.

How many times have I neglected opportunity because what I am doing works? A new place to throw balls for the dogs? This is the place I use the *Chuck-it*. Period. Can I free myself from time a bit? My rigid mentality tracks the quickest means to check off "done". I almost missed the blackberries through the tennis balls.

I'm a creature of habit and comfort zones. If it works, don't change it. The only problem is life loses the zest of *hidden treasures* when we lose our spontaneity. Just ask Sam

I will lead the blind by ways they have not known, along unfamiliar paths I will guide them...

~ Isaiah 42:16

Dear Lord, grant me vision to explore my world today and trek unforged paths that branch off the beaten track of my routines. Open my eyes and clear my mind so I grasp opportunity before me, and discover life beyond and between my lists of to do's. Teach me spontaneity, new routes and new words for common occurrences. Thank you for the great gift of the present. I am seeking hidden treasures.

Keeping Up with the Boneses

"Sammy's my pumpkin and he was born on Dogoween!" I crooned to Sam and lavished a few strong rubs on the back end of his yellow-orange coat, his favorite scratching spot. It was early morning and he was up with a heavy thump-jump off the bed. Benji lay undisturbed, curled and content in his dreams.

We don't need costumes for our annual festive Candyland night. Sam can frighten anyone with his loud bark and Benji has a readymade costume—the markings on his black-and-white schnauzer face resemble a raccoon.

Tonight's sound symphony performed by laughing cowboys and Jedi warriors, giggling princesses and ballerinas, clowns and monsters will crescendo on our porch. Cued from approaching voices, Benji's blaring barks heightened by Sam's swashbuckling tail will synchronize with candy-grubbing neighborhood kids. Toting the goodie basket, we will fling open the front door before the kids have a chance to ring the bell and holler, "Trick or Treat" choruses followed by "Woof and Yip" echoes. That's how we will celebrate Sam's birthday. He will be the first to greet everyone at the door, up close and personal. It's a real doggie delight.

Yep, dogs are delighted by people events as much as people are delighted by doggie events.

Today I spoke with my good friend about her little "Pookie," a nickname for her diva girl, a Maltese.

"Yesterday was Pookie's first birthday," Cheryl announced on the phone.

"Oh really, what did you do?"

"We had the neighbor dogs over for her first Birthday Paw-Tea. My husband bought some treats at The Barkery."

"Oh," I laughed, imagining the drooling party guests.

"One of my neighbors brought over a little striped blue-and-yellow visor for Pookie." Cheryl laughed. She momentarily left me and I heard her whisper some sweet something's to her fluffy girl on the other end.

"Are you going to use it?" I asked puzzled, remembering another friend with twin terriers. She puts doggles on her pets so the wind won't hurt their eyes when they poke their heads out of the car windows.

"Well, I might in the summer, because she's very fair," Cheryl explained. Maltese have such white hair and pink skin, that they can actually sunburn."

"Wow. That is amazing," I said, wondering if Pookie would wear a visor. "When we took Benji to the snow, minutes elapsed before my little Houdini escaped the four small snow boots we laced on his paws to protect them from snow. It seems he's content with the birthday suit God gave him."

Cheryl, a first-time dog owner, seemed to have an

edge over me of what's up in dog world. I checked my uneasiness and the twinge of hesitation when I praised her dogformation.

"You are learning a lot about dogs."

"Yes, I am." She chuckled.

It was time for me to save face as a clued-in dog world news reporter.

"I heard there are four dog shops to a corner in Newport Beach—almost as many dog shops as gas stations."

"Yes, it is known as a dog spot," Cheryl added. "There are dogs everywhere. They even pierce their dog's ears so they can wear little diamonds."

"No way!" I imagined a doggie tattoo parlor as the next rage.

"My sister said they have a pet place in San Francisco where owners go for drinks and appetizers with their dogs—Yappy Hour."

"You're kidding?" I stated, outdone again.

It seems the dog world is growing exponentially, and canines are becoming our newest recognized citizens. Dogs are certainly jumping up the status ladders in America. Recently I read that some employers in Australia give one week paternity leave to welcome a new pet home. One evening my brother called after watching the news, to report the latest in Japan.

"The Japanese consider their dogs as partners. Their dog standards and behaviors are like nothing you've ever seen!"

"Well, my dogs are my partners, too," I retorted,

thinking how Sam and Benji, my partners, just accompanied me back from our daily exercise outing.

"No, you don't understand. It's really like they consider their dogs partners in life! Owners purchase software 'bowlingual' to understand what their pets are trying to say—and stress patches to determine their anxiety level—for starts."

"Wow, that seems excessive."

Sammy and Benji are nothing extraordinary, except of course to me. They are ordinary dogs with ordinary lives. I listen to Benji talk when he brushes against the drapes, paws my arm, or yips incessantly. I listen to Sam when he barks, whines or groans. Or backs his rear into my leg. I know when they're anxious by their tell-tale looks or sounds. And I know they settle down quickly if tossed a treat from their favorite bag of bargain rawhides.

We live a simple life with as little technology as possible. Gadgets mean manuals and manuals stress me out. Sam and Benji have enough agitation waiting for me. Often, they rumble and prance around the living room, leashes dangling and ready, whimpering from delayed gratification while I crisscross different rooms of the house distracted from our outing. They would rather have their walk earlier than wait for me to fidget trying to figure out something electronic. No, my boys won't care what trendy item or activity we don't indulge in—as long as I remember their birthday treat.

This Dogoween we will again focus on the kids' costumes, not theirs. I doubt my boys will be sashaying down a catwalk anytime soon. They may never know how to use their words but they know how to get my attention. Even if the day comes they can browse dog. com for the latest proper care and feeding of canines, I doubt it will change their lives.

They seem to grasp contentment far more than we do. They revel in routine, grateful to be stroked, fed and to play a bit every day. To have a corner for sleep, whether in the garage or on the bed. And thrive in the simple life practicing animal instincts and sometimes gross habits. It's never our Bowser's keeping up with the Boneses. They know what's important. It's their masters trying to keep up with the Joneses.

Better one handful with tranquility than two handfuls with toil and chasing after the wind.
~ Ecclesiastes 4:6

Thank You, Lord, for the opportunity to enjoy events with our critters in small ways and the joy they can bring to children and adults as we celebrate life.

Thank You that our pets don't know the difference between carrots and pastries or diamonds and paper. Keep our lives as grounded and satisfied with simple treats and pleasures as theirs are. And from keeping up with the Boneses.

Beyond the Blinds

Benji loves to watch what's going on. He is a *watch* dog. Sammy is a guard dog who is called to attention by the watch dog. Sam's favorite spot to sleep is against the hills I painted on the walls by the front door. There he lies for hours, peacefully snoring and grunting in a side-lying position, whether the door is closed or open.

Not Benji. If the door is open he is Herr Vigilante, stationed at his post centered evenly between the door-frames—ears wired to the closest satellite—alert and on task. His mission is to detect movement of man or beast and to squeak and squawk at the first appearance of life beyond our borders. At his warning, the guard dog rouses. So do his master's protective instincts.

When the door is closed, Benji props himself on the couch in front of the living room window. Recently, Benji perched on the far right end. His head leaned as far to the right as he could stretch his legs. The living room blinds were closed except the right-side blind. He tried to see as much as he could from his limited view through one narrow pane.

"Benji, I'll give you a great view," I laughed realizing his restricted vision of the front yard limited his ability to provide proper surveillance. Even as I began to open the blinds to the middle pane he maneuvered for a better position and stopped dead center. Grinning I walked away. Looking back I noticed the far left blind was still closed.

"You think you see the whole picture Benji?" Thoughts fluttered in my mind. There is another part of the picture you're still not getting.

Isn't that what it is like with our lives? We strain to see everything we can, especially if we're the hyper vigilant, watch-dog type personality. Sometimes God leaves the blinds closed. In fact, many times. We can't figure out what's happening out there, beyond the blinds, and we want to know how it will affect us.

Why can't we just lie down and let the world go by, like Sam—and let the adrenaline flow in minor doses, when necessary? It's not our nature. We know provision is there. When it's time to be fed—we will be fed. Most of us have never missed a meal, yet we demand to know where the next meal is coming from and how it will be provided.

Recently my friends, Cindy and Rick, had to move from the home they had rented for many years because the owner decided to sell the house. God's timing confused my friends. With so many foreclosures it was difficult to find rentals. They struggled inwardly.

Rick bucked the owner and lost. "God, what is the purpose of this? The timing couldn't be worse!" Reluctant and resigned they began house hunting. The process of securing the rental began with prayer.

"We need to be praying to find a home," Rick announced to their children one night.

"Dad, that's your responsibility," their teenage daughter Lindsay retorted.

"No, we're a family and we're all in this together."

Days later, on a walk with her girlfriend, Lindsay saw a house with a "For Rent" sign on the front. She stopped, clicked a picture with her cell phone and sent it stat to her dad, texting him additional information.

"The rest was a blur, it happened so fast!" Cindy smiled, sharing how everything fell in place like a jigsaw puzzle.

The owners chose them among many when it was discovered they had numerous mutual business connections. "My wife wants your family to have the house." The owner grinned. "And, you can write the lease for as long as you want."

Two months later they had a different story. "This is our miracle house," Cindy gushed yesterday. "God gave us a nicer home in a better location than we had before. We rejoiced over God's goodness, amazed again how He always knows the complete picture—reminded that we must trust His perspective over ours.

"It's just like Benji's view on the couch," I told Cindy. "We can try so hard to prepare ourselves for intrusions, disturbances and unforeseen circumstances. We get upset when change rocks our world, not understanding the full view."

God chooses to leave the blinds closed. He asks us to trust Him, believing we are safe and everything will be okay. Even if He gives us a bigger view and we settle into feeling more secure—there's always that other unopened blind. We never have the full perspective of our lives. Just like Benji still learns to trust me, so we learn to trust God for what we can see—and what we can't.

Let him who walks in the dark, who has no light, trust in the name of the Lord and rely on his God.

~ Isaiah 50:10

Dear Lord, thank You for guiding our lives according to Your plan even when we don't see the big picture. Help us to trust You instead of allowing fear and doubt to cloud our vision. Open the eyes of our heart to see Your perspective and live each day at peace as we choose to watch events unfold before us with faith all will be well.

Doggie Seconds

"Just a second Sam." I ignored his whines and shuffled through the pile of papers in my writing room having decided today was the day to organize and push procrastination aside. Benji sat at alert assuming watchdog position at the living room window.

Mmm. Mmm. Sam whined.

"I know, we'll go for a walk in a second." He turned and walked out of the office swishing his hairy bat-tail from side to side. *Ker plop.* Deep in the piles of my life, I ignored his loud nonverbals.

Mmm. MMMM. An hour late his moans started up the music scale. Benji's barks escalated at the window.

"Okay Sam, in a doggie second we're going for a walk." I tossed another paper in the circular file, assuring him a walk was still on my mind, maybe on the back burner—but it would happen.

Days like this I don't look at the clock, I simply look out the window. Finally, at some perfect spot in the day, when the rays dance on the trees and I am tired of paperwork, it happens. The thought, *what a beautiful time to walk right now,* becomes a force that pushes me out from under the piles. The street clear of work traffic and the clean outside air powerfully beckons me.

"Time to get the leashes!" Sam sprung to all fours quick as lightning from his slumber, clipping my heels as I headed to gather shoes and plastic bags. Benji leapt like a frog from his post and trotted up behind Sam. They were both *insto-walk* ready to join the otherworld that paraded our streets.

But just as I was heading to the door I was sideswiped by my ignored hunger and a phone call I haven't made. Once again the dreaded words tumbled from my mouth.

"Just a little bit longer guys." Heading to the office with my food, I passed the dogs, ignoring Benji's frown, disgruntled sigh, and thump. Sam repositioned himself at the front door again, plopping his jaws like a sandbag over his crisscrossed paws.

"One little doggie second," I coaxed hoping for some mutual agreement, pretending it was fine by them.

Woof, woof. I looked down at Sam's glaring eyes and flaring pink nose—and then at the clock. Okay, it *was* Sam's dinner time and my pile was scattered beyond the realm of organized. One quick glance out the darkened winter window and I acquiesced.

"It's okay guys, we're going now." *I wish I left earlier,* but things were too disheveled and I was trying to finish whatever. This time, I placed the gentle leaders over each anxious dog nose and we headed out the front door—none too soon after the doggie second I promised.

Doggie seconds, as my dogs wait for me, seem relative to the divine perspective of time reflected in the verse, "a thousand years to man is like one day to God." I think the boys must have felt like I was never going to take them out. I feel like that when I'm waiting on God and it seems like God's never going to pull through— like meeting my mate.

I started praying to get married at nineteen. By the time I was thirty, I was whining and waiting. At forty-four, *this time for sure God*—turned to another prayer vigil at the window of surrender as others walked down the aisle to marriage. When I turned fifty, another false start followed by disappointment—*maybe it will never happen*. I rested in the hallway of hope, resigned but listening for the voice of my Master. One day eight months ago God spoke, "Okay, get ready. We're walking."

On the other side of God's day, I can feel like my whole life is going by, much the way my doggies probably felt when the afternoon shadows began to fall and they could see the sun setting. In their minds it must be like…*Now, what is she doing?* As it turned out I was just finishing up some other business, well aware we would get out.

Scampering now around moonlit streets, we captured the colorful lights and delighted in a neighborhood that was just beginning to celebrate our favorite time of the year. I couldn't help but think if we had left earlier we would have missed the glowing giant penguins and snowmen that smiled and waved at us and the reindeer's nod as we passed by.

"This is the perfect time for a winter walk, even though we had to wait a bit, eh boys?"

They cantered next to me, chests high, eyes beaming as we strolled by the Christmas lights.

"A doggie second can seem like a long time, but when we're enjoying the special moments now, isn't it worth the wait?" I don't think they heard me they were so mesmerized by the delightful surroundings. In fact, I think they forgot about the wait—just like I had.

For a thousand years in your sight are like a day that has just gone by, or like a watch in the night.

~ Psalm 90:4

Lord, my dogs always come home content and happy no matter how long they have to wait for their walks. Help me to be content with the answers You have given me in life—from the home that shelters us, to the Dogmobile that drives us safely from point A to point B.

Thank You for answering so many prayers and listening to my longings day in and day out. Help me to trust You better with new challenges ahead, realizing that unlike me—You are wise and deliberate in choosing when to answer and how. And You always choose the right time laced with surprises.

Samson's Turning Tide

I climbed back into the car after our 2:00 am gas fill up, dog stretch time, on our return home from Big Sur Pfeiffer Beach. A pleasant weekend outing turned Twilight travesty.

Sam's first day on the dog beach--and he humps not only a dog, but two children half his size. I apologized to the first parent of a little boy, after he fumed, "This is really abnormal" (over his brother's laughter). I promised to call the vet when I returned home.

Later at another part of the beach, it happened again in a flash while both dogs romped around me and I talked with an old friend.

"I'm so disappointed in Sam," I choked looking over my shoulder at my friendly Lab watching me, sitting silent in the back seat. Memories of the afternoon were still fresh. I heard the little girl crying, clinging to her mother for comfort after Sam, double her size, clung to her. My apologies felt as airless and empty as the windblown sand.

My friend listened with compassion to my confusion. How I raised him responsibly as the owner of an extra-large breed, so he would be good around kids and small animals. I even paid for a purebred Lab this time, to avoid any mean streaks like my last mixed Rot/Lab exhibited. Sam had varied experiences, tons of affection, attention and exercise. I never worried about him. That is, until today.

"I don't trust him around kids anymore, I feel like I'm distancing myself from Sam. "Shocked my sweet Sammy would try to dominate a child, I replayed the troubled mom checking under her little daughter's shirt for scratches while I firmly pressed Sam's face in the sand. My yells overpowered the pounding surf fifty feet away. I didn't know my own dog—this beast I sat on.

This is what my friends must feel when their kids blow it. I recalled recent conversations with scared parents, friends whose wayward adolescents were going through some werewolf metamorphosis. Although I'd done everything I could to prevent bad behavior, I couldn't control this. I bought Sam as a seven-week-old pup, and provided him with hundreds of experiences around kids and other dogs. He received his grad certificate from PetSmart training class at three months and was "fixed" at six months. Every week people commented, "He's such a sweet dog."

"Yes, I'm the lucky one." I've smiled inside and out, joyful to own a big dog I could trust around kids and small animals.

"Denise, you could get sued," my friend cautioned today when we walked away from the latter catastrophe.

"I know." Although reassured the little girl was physically alright, I felt sad, not only for my ill-behaved pet, but for the trembling little girl and her concerned mom.

"I was bit by a big dog when I was a kid," my friend shared as she drove. "I was traumatized for years."

"I know; I saw kids at the hospital for facial bites." I stopped to pray. "Please God, don't let this little girl have nightmares about this, or long-term dog fears."

Oddly enough, a year ago friends thanked me for letting Sam come and visit with their four young boys who were terrified of dogs, especially big ones. Years earlier, their dad was bitten by a large dog in front of the first-born toddler. The fear had traveled down through all the brothers. They grew to love Sam. He made such an impact in their lives, they own a dog today.

Today, I have a new compassion for parents, whether of dogs or kids, whose little charges display aberrant behavior. I have a better grasp of God's feelings toward his children in Jeremiah 2:21 *"I had planted you like a choice vine of sound and reliable stock. How then did you turn against me into a corrupt wild vine? The stain of your guilt is still before me."* I am forced to look at Sam differently than I did before he overpowered these children. He is guilty and I am disappointed.

What is the good that comes from this? Sam will be a good "bad example" for the kids at Juvenile hall. I will share with them that the freedoms we've been given are to bring blessing, joy or growth to others around us. Once we use our freedom to inflict terror or harm, in Sam's case dominance and intimidation, we lose the freedom to express ourselves. Freedom carries responsibility—Sam is now restricted.

I need to be a responsible dog owner. I am Sam's

master just as God is my master, my Lord. Hopefully we learn, by the time we've reached maturity, what benefits those around us and what good manners looks like. Our freedom is limited by our own goodness and integrity.

Sam blew it. I love him, but I will not trust him to freely roam in public areas anymore. Breaking trust is difficult for those who love and influence us. They can feel like they missed something even if they didn't– it was simply our impetuous bad choice. That is the message of Sam's crisis to us—a lesson to learn from.

Of course, Sam's a dog. I don't know if he will ever realize why he will be on-leash more now. And I can't give him a second chance, because I don't know his reason as a dog!

But hopefully, for kids at Juvenile Hall and grown-up kids, the reason for his restriction will sink deep inside of conscience and heart. Humans have a second chance. We are created in the image of God, the God who gives second chances. We are luckier than Sam will be. And Sam is still one lucky dog, because I am a good human master.

My son, don't be angry when the Lord punishes you. Don't be discouraged when he has to show where you are wrong. Let God train you, for he is doing what any loving father does for his children.

~ Hebrews 12:5, 7 (TLB)

Thank you, God, for guiding me with wisdom circumstance by circumstance as I continue to learn how to be a responsible owner and adjust my dog rearing to Sam's recent behaviors. Help me control the controllable. I want to be courteous to my community and keep Sam away from those vulnerable to his impulsive instincts.

May Sam's whines from a tether never woo me to allow him to run free when it could put someone at risk. Keep me from denial of our new normal, vigilant for Sam's benefit and my own. Help me accept reality and stay strong in making the best decisions for Sam.

Seasons Change

"What's the matter Benji?" En route to the kitchen on a writing break, I bent down and tousled Benji's head resting on his furry paws, His bone lay untouched a foot away. His eyes stared straight ahead, not even glancing up at my touch.

Could he be depressed? I wondered after reading an article about dogs with behavior changes that required medications. *I must keep an eye on him.*

Depression. I used to keep a big "I" on the refrigerator that stood for *interest. When a person loses interest in things that they normally enjoy, it is a sign of depression.* It was a personal alert I used while revolving through some difficult and prolonged seasons of work, night-shift and relationship challenges and transitions over a decade of my life.

When I noticed my interest bridging zero, something needed to change. It might mean admitting I needed immediate change for work—to work. It might be I needed courage to address relationship issues and quit stuffing my feelings. Or that I must bridge apathy to pursue help and wise counsel by refusing to tolerate boredom or insanity by running a circular endurance test. Pan for perspective. Find humor. Create. Center on the important—not the urgent.

Now my little dog seemed like he could be labeled soon if something didn't change. The past two weeks his morning watch-dog post—the couch by the front window—stood vacant.

"Benji, look!" I pulled the shades up every morning, offering him the coveted sentry position at the window. He would stare at me from across the room, his mouth fixed in a classic-Benji frown, rigid as a stuffed Eeyore plush pet. "Don't you want to look outside?" His lack of motion and emotion spoke volumes.

This morning we piled into the car to pick up a friend at the hospital. I calculated the time and knew the recent temperature drop meant the dogs could come on a ride-about today. While driving, I glanced at the little face below me, intently observing the view beyond our cozy Dogmobile cockpit. Benji's eyes shone transfixed on the road ahead. His lips curved up; he was smiling. He sat on the console, his legs tucked solidly under him, like a deer in navigator position.

Instead of the air conditioner, the windows were lowered welcoming the cool breeze which circulated through our car. Sammy's nose poked up sniffing and twitching outside the back rear window. *The air is stirring again*, I thought recalling yesterday's discovery, a small pile of gold leaves clustered in the corner of our front porch. The seasons are changing.

Benji transfixed, looked like his old self, alert, alive and interested. It has been a long summer, a dry, muggy season—so hot, the dogs are inside all the time, except for our early morning walks.

"I think Benji is sick of summer," I smiled at my little one. His eyes met mine. He repositioned himself and settled peacefully on the console. "You're ready for a change of seasons, aren't you Benji?" Patting his head fondly, I promised, "We'll be going out more now."

When we arrived at the hospital, my friend hopped out of the wheelchair, opened the passenger door and threw her bag on the floor.

"Can we leave now? I have felt so cooped up for the last twenty-four hours I could hardly stand it!"

I looked at Benji. His mouth stayed fixed—in a smile.

Praise be to the name of God forever and ever; wisdom and power are his. He changes times and seasons. ~ Daniel 2:20–21

Thank You, God, that You know our limits and how much we can endure. Bolster us to wait patiently when the tunnels in life are long and dark and the light seems so far away. Grant us courage and endurance to make it through the long difficult passages knowing long Indian summers will always pass into the colors of fall just as You have planned.

Groans of Love

I stood on the river rocks praying while watching this slimmed-down version of Sam, my yellow Lab, wade in the mild current. Cottonwood pollen floated above us. A white Egret perched undisturbed on one leg in the sun upstream. Benji, my little puppy-cut schnauzer, trotted by gripping an old salmon skeleton five times the size of his mouth. My heart felt as dry as that fishbone.

Just this time the day before, I stood in my bathroom and groaned. It sounded much like Sam when he couldn't hop up on the bed—and I couldn't help him. He was too big. Startled by my own groan, something had clicked—the scripture in Romans 8:26. *In the same way the Spirit helps us in our weakness. We do not know what we ought to pray for, but the Spirit himself intercedes for us with groans that words cannot express.*

That strange sound coming from my pained heart— hearing my pet's groan—is what happens when the Holy Spirit, our Comforter, groans for us. He expresses the distress we feel when we have no words, just as I subconsciously expressed the distress I felt for my Sam.

I kicked the fishbone out of Benji's mouth just as a tune rocked my cell phone. A Chicago area code.

"Hi, friend, how's Sam?"

"Oh he's the same," I answered the familiar voice of DeeAnne. "Not eating. Throwing up. Losing weight. The tests come back this week."

"How are you?" she asked. "I've been praying for you."

"Everything triggers me. Usually, when we hit the streets near the river access, he's barking so loud I'm trying to quiet him down. On the way here Sammy's whine was weak and low. I cry a lot."

I described the previous two weeks—then asked about her two dachshunds. One died suddenly of pancreatic cancer. The other suffered for a year with food allergies so severe, she had sores and weight loss—until they discovered she was even sensitive to the organic foods DeeAnne carefully prepared.

"Wheat, chicken, dairy…" she continued. "She would lick her paws constantly."

"Really?" I perked up as I pictured Sammy's recent on-again, off-again bouts licking his paws. "Sammy just started licking his paws this past month. He had little sores between his wedges. But I thought it was from sinking in the snow when he has gone to the mountains a couple times. Right now he's stopped."

"Frankie had sores between her paws on and off for a year," DeeAnne moaned. "She was miserable and licked them constantly."

"What does she eat now?" I asked.

"Rice, potatoes, carrots, broccoli-slaw. There's one dry food with yams and fish she can eat."

"No kidding?" I looked at Sam, still wading and peaceful. "There was a food on the internet yesterday produced by California Natural for dog allergies with sweet potato and salmon. I was just going to buy some at the Western Feed Store on the way home."

"Yes, that's the only thing Frankie will eat!"

"I was going to try boiling rice in chicken broth for flavor today—now, I think not!"

"Frankie reacts to any poultry product, even broth," DeeAnne sighed.

I felt a surge of energy much like the current, gliding down the main branch of the river to the east of our little inlet.

DeeAnne and I prayed. Gratefulness filled my heart.

Walking back to the car, I watched the sun dance off Sammy's golden coat as he led the way. Benji swayed close beneath his belly, distracted by every creature and insect on the nature trail. I felt God's love surrounding me. He had heard me in the bathroom and met me at the river. The glow of the day bathed my skin as the promise of tomorrow rose again in my soul.

Show me your ways, O Lord, teach me your paths; guide me in your truth and teach me, for you are God my Savior, and my hope is in you all day long.
~ Psalm 25:4–5

🐾

Dear Lord, thank You for caring about my animals, just as You care for me. Thank You for helping me experience the depth of Your love for me, by knowing the depth of my love for my dog. Please guide me in this unfamiliar territory to believe that You can do miracles. Even today, restore my hope.

When I have no answers, please guide me to the right place. Grant me the knowledge I need to care for my pet the best way I can through the wisdom You give me. I ask for Your help, humbly aware that You are my Creator and that You created my dog.

Indecision

"Benji, get out of the middle," I often say to my little guy as he blocks my attempts to shut the door.

Next my voice rises, "Do you want to stay in or do you want to go out?" He usually continues to stand there, at least until I'm unhappy. This is better than when he stands in the pitch black garage at night while I hold the door open and begin turning into a Popsicle.

First I say in my sweetest tone, "Do you want to come in, Benji-bo?" And, of course, he stands there unflinching and nonresponsive. "Benji, do you want to come in? I repeat louder, adding a freezer-burn dimension to my voice, as Benji stares at the threshold of the door. He knows and I know if I take a step forward, he will just move backward.

He stares at me as if to say, "Don't make me come in. I haven't made up my mind yet."

Thank goodness, Sammy is a different story. Almost always, given an open door, he walks right through. He seldom chooses to stay out. If he does, he is so un-annoying. He just turns and heads out the garage.

Maybe he'll turn toward me.

"Are you sure you don't want to come in, Sam?" I'll ask.

Then he may give me *the look*, a certain yes as he continues to the yard. Or, if he wants to come in, he just steps right by me at a quick pace and heads where he wants to go. Sammy is so much easier to read than Benji. He is a direct communicator. He knows what he wants.

But Benji. If I can't coax him in or catch him, I know what will happen. Why? Because it happens all the time. After I shut the door and settled into whatever I'm doing, as soon as I'm comfortable as a Popsicle wedged into a freezer—99% of the time he'll begin pawing the door to come in.

His little nails start on the door or sliding glass door, the chalk on the blackboard scratch, over and over. It drives me crazy.

Now, I get why friends have become upset with me playing board games...taking forever to make a move either direction, because I'm rehearsing all options and effects. Or trying to pick a menu item at a restaurant when everything looks so good. Often, I've whittled it down to two or three tantalizing dishes—then request the waiter to pick one for me—or my eating companion, when I'm really stuck.

I'm sure the blank look doesn't help either when they have raised their voices and asked me again, what I want, what I need and if I need some help (thinking I didn't hear them the first time).

I did.

I'm thinking—just like Benji.

Don't grumble against each other, brothers, or you will be judged. The judge is standing at the door!

~ James 5:9

Thank You, Lord, for reminding me the things that irritate me about others are often things I do myself. Help me to be slow to speak and slow become angry. I pray for patience for myself and offer it to those who need it today.

Terms of Endearment

"Yesterday Bruno jumped onto my lap while I was writing," my friend Beth relayed. "But, I had to put him back on the floor because I couldn't type well." Beth rubbed her jaw.

"Later, when I bent down to pet him, he sprung up with all his strength—right into my jaw! Even though he's a tiny Yorkshire terrier, twelve pounds of full force still hurt a lot. Today I named him, "my little jawbreaker'."

I smiled. My dogs have also earned names that change as often as a scrolling desktop screen. They occur so randomly they even amuse me—like yesterday's term of enticement.

"Over here Harriet Rabbit"…"Come on, my Pink-nosed Pig," I cajoled, herding Benji and Sam from Mom's front yard to the cars open doors.

Benji ran by pushing his rear off from both legs—hopping. Since his tail is docked, and he has soft curly fur, add the stump to the hop and from behind he is a black and silver hare. The name Harriet Rabbit just slipped out—it seemed to fit.

Sammy will eat anything from tire-treaded McDonald's leftovers to Kleenex and socks. "pink-nosed pig" is an appropriate name for him in street scavenger mode.

Benji pushes a full dish of food under the recliner, under the table, against the wall. "He doesn't eat his food; he just pushes his plate around," Mom complained after she doggie-sat recently. My little "shove-l" uses his nose constructively.

The only time Sammy is disinterested in food is when tennis balls are around. He picks up one, two or three and hoards them in his mouth—bulging cheeks like a "chipmunk" packs acorns.

Benji practices resistance, my daily frustration. Whether I ask, instruct, or command him to climb into the car or come in the house—he does just the opposite—my "ever-ready rebel."

Unlike Sammy who is usually pretty obedient because he aims to please me—my "pleasant pumpkin."

Sammy can't contain his emotions. Ever. Even strangers know what he's thinking. If I manage to keep him away from guests, he reluctantly assumes half-sit position, derriere off the floor, and wriggles so hard the earth moves under his tail. A social animal who loves attention he is Shrek's "Donkey" in Lab disguise. If he could talk, I'm sure I'd be as annoyed as the green Ogre.

Benji barks ferociously when visitors arrive, warning to stay away…then retreats. He distances himself under a chair or table, once the intruders step inside. The ruff of my "Cowardly Lion" only induces amusement in our trespassers.

I have met people who addressed their kids

affectionately, calling them everything from pumpkin to pistol. My stepdad called me "peanut" because I am small-framed, and I called him "bean" because his last name was Fava and he was round. I missed my nickname when he left for Heaven.

Nicknames portray a bit of truth, however they are coined among friends and family circles. I love to use them in fun, but some I've accrued haven't always denoted traits.

Once I sat across from a nurse manager as we reviewed a work incident in which I hadn't restrained myself any better than Sam—but had dismissed my behavior.

"I'm not a machine-gun, I'm a pistol. One outburst and it's over." I fully expected her to applaud my response toward a very aggravating, verbally assaultive co-worker.

"Well, a pistol is not welcome here," she corrected me, cutting away my excuses.

So we spoke in terms of alignment. I needed to switch gears how I expressed my frustrations, and draw boundaries maturely, even with the most impossible of humanity.

Although difficult, I needed to refrain myself and heed my Master's voice, just as Sam and Benji need to obey my voice in circumstances that induce excitement or agitation in their little psyches. If I ignored my boss, and more importantly my God, and reacted however I wanted, I could damage myself and the person I bombarded with my anger.

Little Jawbreaker exerted one more push from self-will and impatience. If he had just waited a little longer, maybe Beth's pat would have calmed him until the timing was right to sit on her lap once again. Then, he could have enjoyed the birds-eye view out their back window and received her fond approval.

Instead, he injured her accidentally and he walked "around in a daze" the next day—from a possible minor concussion—the consequences of impatience.

Lessons come hard in life. Names are earned sometimes, and sometimes not. Hopefully, we drop the negative ones we have accumulated and acquire complimentary ones from our positive behavior. Hopefully, we grace people we like with affectionate terms of endearment, in good humor and from good intentions—not labeling them in harmful ways, slandering their character and conjuring shame.

And just like my *little black button* and *my big pink button* know, terms of endearment convey acceptance and love—even as we work on becoming better versions of ourselves.

A good name is more desirable than great riches, to be esteemed is better than silver or gold.
~ Proverbs 22:1

Lord, thank You for the constructive criticism of those around me, even when it is hard to hear. Help me to build a good name by excellent character and protect me from my own stubborn pride and impatience that affects me and others, and can even disappoint you. Amen.

The Ball is in the Big Dog's Court

Grrr. Grrr. I glanced over my shoulder and caught a glimpse of silver-black hair in my periphery, and the edge of a green ball—the exposed part of a tennis ball. The rest was tightly clamped in big dog's canine jaws. Neither Benji nor the claws of a King Crab could get that ball—or any ball—out of Sam's mouth.

"Come here Benji," I dipped my hand in the baggie and threw a few dog food pebbles, Benji's treats, on the front seat. He quickly hopped over the console next to me and chomped quietly on his morsels.

"Sam, drop the ball" Minutes ago, before leaving the parking lot, I had tried to coax Sam to let go so I could *Chuck-it*. But lately, when Sam retrieved the ball he wouldn't let it go. Benji and I faced the raging waters of Sam's possessiveness.

"Benji?" I eyed my little guy intently staring at the ball in Sam's mouth. The nuggets only pacified him briefly. My voice was stern. "Don't even think about it. The ball is always in Sam's court. That's just the way it is."

The word *court* reminded me of my attorney's call this very morning. He explained away everything I had gathered for him—what I thought was fuel for my legal battle.

"I know it's horrible and unfair," he sighed. "Don't you remember when I told you, they won't include..." He listed the items my adversaries would not compensate me for—just about everything on the list I had sent him yesterday. I hoped the case was coming to a close, but he left me with the parting words— "The ball is in their court."

Remembering, I spoke with mixed emotion to my little dog. "The ball is always in the big guy's court, Benji." He did not comprehend he was much too small to wrest that ball out of the grip of Sam's chompers.

I began speaking to Benji and to myself.

"But that doesn't mean you can't enjoy your stuffed animals and run in the parking lot to sniff and whiff new discoveries. While Sam struts around with the ball glued to the roof of his mouth, enjoy your moments. You just have to let go of wanting that ball.

The ball will always be in Sam's court just like in this case I'm facing, the ball is always in the defendant's court—their four attorneys against my one. I could pull and tug for what is mine or share the territory we both occupied. I didn't have to sit and whine or lose what I had or could discover in my venture, anymore than Benji had to be miserable just because he'd never have the ball.

When we arrived home Sam ran in the house and lay on the floor his treasure resting securely between his molars. Benji trotted into the hall and settled by his ragged grey elephant and I went to get dressed and ready. It was time to go to court.

Lord, you have assigned me my portion and my cup; you have made my lot secure. The boundary lines have fallen for me in pleasant places; surely I have a delightful inheritance. ~ Psalm 16:5–6

Thank You, God, for helping me let go of the inequities in life, and work with what I have to enjoy…the world around me. Even when bad stuff happens to good people and the big guys always seem to win, remind me that whatever I don't have, I don't need. There are plenty of gifts all around me to be thankful for.

Leave It

"Sam, leave it!"

Sam tugged me toward the hot street as he clung fiercely to his position and slurped the last sticky bit-of-something smashed into the black street.

"Sammy, that's disgusting."

Little Benji stood at my side with a silent frown.

Too late, we headed up the street again. Just as we sauntered by the ivy patch lining thirty feet at the corner house, Sam's nose started twitching, scanning the ivy like a metal detector. Suddenly he pitched his head down deep into green leaves, his hair furrowed in a ridge down his large yellow back.

"Leave it, Sam!" I repeated the command as he whipped his head up. Something gray dangled in his mouth. I scrunched my eyes. *I hate rodents.*

"*Aahhhh!*" Shaking, I screamed, "Leave it! Leave it!" I tugged the leash like Popeye after a can of spinach. Sammy loosened his jaw and dropped the unlucky sucker with a wire tail. My mind raced. The tension only eased when I recalled his recent rabies vaccination.

I had to call a friend to unload. "Sammy forgot the command, *leave it*. It's time to reinforce it again."

The next day I dropped treats in the center of the

epoxied garage floor and leashed Sam. We walked around the treats in random figure eights. Initially, Sam tried to grab the morsels as we walked by. Benji frowned, tethered at the corner of the garage, unable to reach us.

"Leave it." I gave Sam's leash a quick tug. "Remember, Sam, when you were a puppy and graduated from the Petsmart training class? You knew 'leave it' but now we have to practice again. You forgot this important command!" After a few rounds and rewards for obedience, Sammy looked up at me, his eyes shining brightly. "Good boy!" I smiled to myself.

How many times has God had to teach me "leave it," and I have forgotten? I have learned to hear His voice, and ignored it in the pull of the moment, without thinking. I happen to be impulsive, like Sammy. Benji stood in the corner watching us. He hardly ate his food, let alone garbage. But Benji needed some reinforcement also. "Benji, you're next." His ears perked up.

Just like Sammy has to relearn "leave it," Benji has to relearn "come." This morning, in a flash like a toddler, he was at the garage door and seconds later materialized down the sidewalk following a lady and her child. "Come, Benji!" I called, amazed at his light speed. He didn't come, so I ran over, quickly scooped him up and carried him back home.

I need to reinforce "come" with Benji, I surmised on our little jaunt back. Sammy can be off leash at times—because he consistently "comes."

Good masters anticipate their dogs' needs and

corresponding commands, aware how important particular ones are to the well-being of their animals.

In a sense, God will do that with us. He allows us to go through situations where we can apply and repeat what we have learned. He reinforces so we continue in the good ground we have gained and maintain control. If we lose ground and begin to coast—we only coast when we're going downhill—He will give us the opportunity to relearn and regain what we have lost.

After a few brief sessions walking Sammy, I already see the difference. And Benji's whipping back around to "come" with treats as a reward. I like to think I'm becoming a new and improved version of myself as I learn to listen to God. Hopefully I am quicker to let go of things that don't benefit me, harmful things, when I hear that voice beckon me to come and follow Him.

Whether you turn to the right or to the left, your ears will hear a voice behind you, saying, "This is the way; walk in it."   ~ Isaiah 30:21

Help me, Lord, to remember the lessons I've learned to "leave it." Remind me what the leave-it things are when I am suddenly tempted to pick them up. Maintain the growth from lessons I have learned in life. Keep me from compromise and slipping from the ground I've gained on some of the uphill treks You have already walked me through.

I trust You will reinforce the strides I have made and that I understand it is for my good that You discipline and guide me. I trust You have my best at heart. I want to be healthy and whole, keeping in stride with You as I follow Your footsteps.

Reflections from the Zoo

One day I watched a young girl walk a mean, muzzled dog shaking its head back and forth on the other side of the street. It's the same girl who lost control of her dog last month when she walked by my house. It's the same dog who wriggled out of his muzzle and his owner's weak grip as Sam, my 110-pound Lab, lay tethered on our front lawn, resting from a recent illness. The brute bit and held Sammy's neck until my friend pulled him off. If it had been my fifteen-pound schnauzer, Benji, he could be dead.

I thought about this over and over. I can worry about little things that never happened, things that could happen again, and things that are happening.

Two years ago, life was a zoo.

One day I stood staring at various shades of dark socks, having difficulty deciphering the color and the ribbings. They each almost matched the other—but didn't. *My life is out of order and I'm lining up socks.* The thought persisted.

So I had stared at six unmatched socks lined up across the foot of my bed, some new, some not. Frustration peaked. *How could their mates disappear so quickly?* It emphasized my life of endless errands, never-ending to-do lists and commitments that fill the twenty-four hours God gives me every day. Almost matching up, but not quite, a lot like my life half the time. The fragmentation comes when my thoughts and my time are in disarray, and from wasting money—like the money I had wasted on these socks.

Looking back, the big problem was my life ledger was out of whack.

I added things on my to-do list without taking anything off. The list got so heavy and lopsided it ended up spinning out of control. Finally at a retreat (that was not a retreat) it all came undone. I was frazzled and disconnected with myself, God, and others on any deep level. Multi-tasking had digressed to multi-fragmenting.

I dropped some of the big things that kept me running, stringing time and purpose along out of sync. Like a broken kaleidoscope, my life had no order, no pattern. A break was due, and it came. When I quit a ministry at church that was in effect a second job, my heart stopped randomly racing.

One night, home late from work, I walked my dogs again by starlight. I stared at a huge moon—silhouetted by pines—glowing over the small hill of a street. Its unearthly appearance pulled me into a God moment.

Suddenly the moon disappeared, clouds eclipsing the spiritual thought that we are to reflect God just like the moon reflects the sun. I stared at a darkened sky. But wait. The moon popped out of the clouds. Once again, I gazed entranced by its beauty.

Maybe that is like our lives really. We reflect God, but then the reflection is hidden by obstacles. Yet it is still there only to reappear again and again. I take the dogs for a fun field outing and end up in the vet's office with a foxtail in Benji's paw. Or, an afternoon is shot cleaning the car and Sam, following a brief trip to the river, during which Sam rolled in stinky dead salmon. And so life moves in ebbs and flows of time, some with purpose, some as waste or empty space. We keep walking through our days looking up watching for the light to reappear.

In time we will rediscover how our lives, like Creation's nightly display, will line up again. God orders our days. He will continue to signal us to let go of worry and focus on watching, waiting and listening for His direction and presence. Matching socks to cover our feet are insignificant compared to the direction of our feet matching and following his leading. He will guide us to worry-free days as we follow Him and trust Him to look after us and our little critters.

But the path of the righteous is like the light of dawn, which shines brighter and brighter until full day.
~ Proverbs 4:18 (RSV)

Father, thank You for the gift of today and the experience of life, whether it reflects a pattern and purpose we value or seeming random chaos or drama we would rather not endure. May we reflect Your greater purpose as we choose to live each day sorting essentials from the non-essentials and removing clutter and disorder—keeping order to the best of our ability.

Grant us wisdom and patience, understanding that many events and days—even in a life well lived— may not make sense. Grant us grace to respond just for today the best way—Your gentler, quieter way—to illuminate the dark rooms of our minds. You are processing our lives through the eyes of an artist, bringing fuller dimension and perspective, using time, dark and light.

Fascinations

"Okay Benji, you can go." As soon as I unclipped my little one's leash he darted out into the grass behind the garbage dumpster. Sammy, roaming free and unhinged, continued thrusting his nose through the eight-inch blades like a rototiller. Now, Benji joined him at the hip in the green field, chomping on a clump of blades after twisting and pulling them free.

I beelined to the giant tree nearby amazed at the width of the trunk. I imagined the rings circling decade after decade to create a beauty like this one.

"This is a heritage tree." I waved my arm to get the attention of the facility worker nearby. A find like this begged to be shared.

"What?" He looked up from his edger.

"This tree is at least sixty years old! Look at the size of its trunk. And it's hidden over here behind the building and garbage dump!"

He shrugged his shoulders and smiled. "It's older than me."

He barely glanced at the gnarled old dinosaur. *Obviously, it doesn't interest him*, I thought, surprised. Sammy and Benji squirmed with excitement running from one patch of grass to the next. Their noses were in high vibrator mode. The grass interested me as little as the tree interested the man in the uniform.

But I smiled at their pleasure, immersed in something that drew their affection, because they were made to smell the odors of fresh grass and the scents of other visitors, it attracted visitors that left their marks on the grass like humans left their marks on the trunk of the tree.

Joy surged through me watching them putter in their wonderland. I knew I could leave them here and they could stay busy for hours.

A memory danced into my mind.

"I never cared about ballet," my pastor said, "until my daughter took an interest in theatre. All of a sudden I sat through musicals and dramatic stage plays simply because she liked it so much. Even if it didn't do anything for me, just to be in a place where she had so much pleasure made it enjoyable for me, too."

And so it is with life. We do the things we need to do to be with the people or critters that we care for so much. Their pleasures become ours, not necessarily the gift itself but what happens to them when they are around their interest.

If they were strangers, or acquaintances, it would not be the same. What gives us the enjoyment is feeling the pleasure of those we care about and watching them light up. Seeing the heightened emotion when they connect a bat or tennis racket with a ball, or finally paint a rock on their canvas that looks like a rock. Or find just the right color for that wall that needed something to brighten up the room.

Yes, those close to our hearts expand our borders and bring opportunity for discovery to our doorstep, if we are open to understanding their fascination, joining them, and following their hearts, too.

The wings of the ostrich flap joyfully, but they cannot compare with the pinions and feathers of the stork. She lays her eggs on the ground and lets them warm in the sand. ~ Job 39:13–14

Lord, please keep us open to the sense of wonder that is around us every day if we step out of our surrounding long enough to marvel at the planet You surround us with. There is so much more in the world of art and science, skies and oceans, plants and animals that we miss during our daily routines.

Thank You for the people and critters around us that pull us into their field of fascination and keep our heads out of the sand.

He's a Keeper

"Oh, hi, Sam! Good boy, Sam." Steve threw the ball, and Sam darted around the ash tree. He groveled on the ground for the lime green tennis ball. "I played fetch with Slate all the time." Steve beamed as he spoke of his half-golden, half-black Lab who had died a couple years before. "He was the most amazing dog."

Steve shared stories of Slate more and more lately as he romped with our pack—Sam, Benji and I.

My doggies responded well to Steve. Sam loved having another big guy like him around. Benji, normally wary and reclusive with anyone until he grew to trust them, had surprised me. When six-foot-three Steve walked in, Benji ran up to Steve's feet and rolled over on his back, all fours up in the air. The only other person I had seen him in that vulnerable position with was my nephew David, dubbed Alpha.

Wow, I thought. When Steve picked him up, Benji licked his lips and seemed to melt in his arms.

Okay, that's a good sign. I tucked these vignettes into my mental file. As time marched on, I became more impressed.

"Sam needs to learn some good manners," Steve stated firmly to me one day in the kitchen after he gave

Sam a treat. Although Sam sat for the dog biscuit, his jaw would quiver and drool. When the treat was offered for his sitting obedience, he immediately chomped his jaws like an alligator. It was a quick draw back to avoid a lost finger. "He can't keep doing this!"

"Oh, he can't help it. He's always done that!" I smiled and patted Sam affectionately. He begged for the carrots from the fridge with waiting eyes. "He's such an eager beaver he doesn't realize he can injure our fingers. I never hand him a treat like I do Benji," I explained to Steve. "Proper Benji, like a little gentleman in his black and silver coat, pulls the biscuit neatly from my hand and trots off with his lollie.

"But Sam…I just throw food in the air and he catches it like Air Bud!" I grabbed a couple carrots and told Sam to sit ten feet away. "Watch!" I nodded to Steve and flipped a baby carrot a few feet above Sam's golden head. He flung up like a frog leaps for a fly and caught it. Another stunning performance.

"Good boy, Sam!" I was pretty proud of his abilities.

Steve was not impressed. "No, he needs to learn to take a treat from your hand."

"He loves food too much and he's always done this. Eight years old is too old for him to start." I winced.

Steve stood by the fridge. Sam sat in front of him, eyes fixed on his hand. Steve's fingers gripped a biscuit. "Gentle, gentle."

"Good luck." I laughed and walked away.

Every time Steve came over, he worked with Sam. Two weeks later, I was not only amused but my respect for Steve escalated. Sam sat in front of Steve and gazed at his open hand holding the biscuit. Sam did not move until Steve stated the phrase "Okay, gentle." Sam touched his nose on Steve's palm and picked the biscuit off his hand.

"I can't believe you taught Sam to do that!" Truly delighted, I tried it myself. Sam repeated the performance.

This was amazing. Steve's patience and command paid off. The dogs loved him. Benji's bark turned into a high screech, his signal for a very special person, whenever Steve arrived. Sam grabbed his ball his usual hospitable way, and Steve always welcomed him back with a gusty "Hi, Sam!" He would pat and rub Sam's extra-large torso as Sam grinned and leaned against Steve's legs.

I watched and remembered. I had dated a man who did not like big dogs—only little ones. He tolerated Sam and his clumsy ways. At one point, he suggested if we were to marry, he could not see Sam in the picture. I remember how sad I felt. Of course the relationship didn't work.

And now, here was a man, a friend, who liked big dogs and liked Sam—even if Sam was a little spoiled. He didn't complain and judge him and leave it at that. He spent time with him and worked with him and made him better. Oddly enough, soon after we started dating, Steve confided, "I never really liked little dogs—but I love Benji! He's the neatest little guy. He's the best." It seemed our small world was nicer with Steve around.

I had brought Sam with me to look at the litter of schnauzer puppies the day I chose Benji. The owner gave me first choice and suggested the puppy with the thickest most beautiful coat. But he cowered from Sam. Benji, the size of a half-pint, moved toward Sam's big pink nose like it was cotton candy. Sam sniffed his tiny body. Benji picked Sam. And Sam picked Benji. Now Benji and Sam were helping me pick my mate.

When special people come into our lives, we don't always know it. I did not know Steve would be part of our menagerie when we met four years earlier. I did not even realize it after dating a few months. But I like to think Sam and Benji knew from the very beginning.

You open your hand and satisfy the desires of every living thing. ~ Psalm 145:16

Thank You, God, for the amazing intuition You give our animals. It is a gift we can rely on and are grateful for. Thank You for the affection and protection they bring us, even when we don't always realize it. And thank You for the gift You have given some people, like my husband, who can work with them and are gifted in training them. It is a wonder to behold.

One Disenchanted Night

"Bark! That will be our new word."

My new groom and I smiled sheepishly over our papaya and bagels on china, the first morning at our bed and breakfast. And our first resolution as newlyweds.

The view overlooking Hilo Bay inspired both of us to be thankful for the opportunity to start a new day—fresh with high hopes riding on understanding and mutual forgiveness. The colorful flowers and ocean breeze provided a stark contrast to the bleak moments and dark words that dampened our moods only hours after landing in our tropical paradise to begin our honeymoon.

God, our master teacher, erased those hurtful words like the black surface of an eraser wipes the board clean for a new learning session. We'd only just begun this adventure, so I had to bring it up once again…to be sure. Especially since I couldn't even remember exactly how it started or what is was all about.

"I'm sorry for being so harsh and not speaking the truth in love. My delivery felt like it took the wind out of your sails. It wasn't kind and I don't want to do that."

My groom looked at me with a sliver of the sadness I saw last night. "I'm sorry for bombarding you with my words," he interjected. Always diplomatic, still his words had flowed steady and persistent like unrelenting rain and eventually drenched me with frustration.

"Yes, I accept your apology." We clicked our ring fingers simultaneously, a gesture of agreement. "Maybe from now on when our words hurt and we need to stop, 'bite' can be an indicator to stop talking."

Our eyes met and smiled in love. Although mature in age, we were unpracticed in expressing requests, aggravations and disappointments with each other, in the close quarters marriage required. We had both lived single and independent for years.

Doused with emotion but lacking accuracy, we had been incorrectly interpreting each other's non-verbal cues—even what we perceived as direct questions and answers. Now we backtracked to re-evaluate any patterns of behavior.

Sometimes we both talked over or interrupted each other—like barking—verbal volume that filled space, created noise, and felt disrespectful.

We needed this pause and reflection to ensure a blissful honeymoon and ten peaceful days traveling together 24/7.

"Barking could be another cue," I thought aloud and winked at my handsome Prince. "Whenever Sammy feels frustrated or confused he begins to bark nonstop. Our emoter (as we call him) does not attempt to restrain his wants, even after we respond to him. Even when we say, "Stop it Sam, we hear you.""

Comic relief buffered our impasse. We were on the same page. Humored by the solution, our spirits lifted knowing we resolved our first marriage spat by changing our approach and halting hurtful words. Two signals—"biting" or "barking"—signified either that word hurts or you're repeating your words and they are getting louder and louder.

Sam, at nine, has seen me through many passages of life. I had leaned on him in some very trying times, unlike any dog I had ever had. My heart burst with love for my new husband and my old Sam, my big yellow affectionado. Again, he was helping me through an important season of my life—marriage and my honeymoon—even though he was at home across the ocean with our dog-sitting family.

Wherever we go, we carry those we love safely embedded deep in our hearts. We carry the lessons they have taught us as a result of our devotion and commitment to them. Lessons God used in our teachable moments, of how to love better in the days and years to come.

Beloved, let us love one another; for love is of God, and he who loves is born of God and knows God.
~ 1 John 4:7 (RSV)

Thank You, God, for the lessons of love we learn through our animals. The patience they develop in us, as we cope with their irritating expressions, causes us to realize the need for greater patience with people in our lives. Grant us grace beyond the noise to hear the needs of those we love, who may express themselves as poorly as we do.

Thank You for the humor we can find in the tensest moments through our pets. Transform us from grudging to forgiving and even forgetting—a great way to start any new day.

Acceptance

"I'm like Sammy!" I grinned as my husband Steve backed away from one of my impulsive hugs.

"Yeah, like Sammy!" His eyes widened in agreement. "I get nervous around Sammy, how to brace myself, so he won't push me and hurt my back."

"You make me afraid of you!" He frowned. "I'm at a huge risk of being knocked out in the next two or three days!"

We laughed that morning highly amused at the truth of his statement.

Soon after, I walked with a friend who was particularly interested how I was adjusting to married life after being single so long.

"I needed Benji to teach me about Steve even before we were married." We walked in stride, Benji ahead of us, his leash in hand.

"What do you mean?

"Well, Sam, my Lab, is an extrovert like me. A bit clumsy with quick movements and a loud bark. How many times have I banged heads with him as his head rises and mine dips to greet each other? Sam was so excited to see us when we returned from our honeymoon, he lumbered into Steve's knee and injured it. He's not real gentle. He gets excited and loves good strong love pats—slaps like football players give each other after a touchdown. He doesn't pause to weigh situations or people real well. He is just out there—impulsive.

"Benji, on the other hand, is very cautious and reserved around people. He is my introvert. He will stare from a distance. You must let him be until he's ready to move toward you."

Benji stopped to smell some bushes.

"Really?" My friend laughed.

"Yes. And he's gentle. He does not respond if you pat him too hard or speak too loudly. He will back away. He demands a soft touch. He's always been like that. Sam can be rustled about and he loves it. The boys wrestle with him, and he craves that attention."

I smiled at my little terrier who trotted on his paws like a dancer light on his feet. "Benji likes even, loving strokes. He'll move his head like a cat against your hand to scratch his ears. If I get too loud or gruff with him, he'll shy away, even from me. I have to earn his trust again. It may take a couple days."

"My son Jake is like that! I thought he just needed to learn to man-up." My friend stopped and looked at me—eyes wide. "But, he's not like my other children. He'll retreat to his room. He doesn't like loud noise. And he winces if I hug him too hard."

"He's like Benji… and my husband. He likes gentle. If you want to be close to him, you will have to be the one to change. That is how it is. To be close to Benji, I've had to change my ways. I'm not as stern with him as Sam. I don't touch him as vigorously as Sam. I have to slow down my movements so I don't startle him and I've had him since he was six weeks old. That's who he is. And God made him like that. Just like Jake. They don't have to change because they can't. That's how God made them. We change if we want to be close to them."

"Wow. I'm going to think about this." My friend spoke hushed with a new perspective of her son.

The talk that day, not so long ago, stayed with me. It amazes me that animals teach us by their very own little personalities and natures the acceptance of others who are not similar to us. I really do believe my gentle miniature schnauzer was my preparation for living with my husband, my gentle giant.

After a disagreement early in our marriage Steve told me, "I don't respond to anger, I respond to gentle." I didn't get it. It took me a while and required some mistakes before I earned his trust. But I would look at Benji and know what I needed to do. It became not so much a puzzlement as a challenge to my thinking.

Why should I change for someone else? Why wouldn't I change for someone else? Especially if I valued the way God made them.

I valued my little schnauzer. I changed my ways for him. I walked slower around him and avoided his feet so he wouldn't be afraid I would step on them. I spoke softer and picked him up with care. Why couldn't I give the same honor to my husband, who asked me to speak softer and be tender with him?

I hoped my friend would re-evaluate her parenting with Jake, too.

If it's one thing Benji can teach others who want to be around him, it's how to be real. To give real acceptance of another who is inherently different from him. He cannot pretend to be anything he's not. He is who he is. Yes, I have been learning for a long time now, how to live with gentle natured creatures, whether they have four legs or two. And I kind of think God planned it that way.

Be completely humble and gentle; be patient, bearing with one another in love. Make every effort to keep the unity of the spirit through the bond of peace.
~ Ephesians 4:2–3

Thank You, Lord, for giving me love for people and animals who are different than me. Help me not only to accept them but to learn new ways and expressions of gentleness, a part of me that seems hidden—I know it is within my capability, too, if I make a conscious effort. Help me to practice gentleness with those You have put in my life.

Barriers

A small black nose and two dark eyes peeked at me through accordion dog gate spanning our bedroom doorway. I felt mean. So many of my friends allow their dogs to sleep with them—but now, Benji, our aging miniature schnauzer, can't even enter our bedroom.

We had potty-proofed the house from our Alzheimer dog. We'd been unsuccessful keeping him in diapers, and belly pads were too small for his large mistakes—too costly for our newly carpeted master bedroom.

"Can't Benji at least be on the throw rug inside the room?" I asked my husband while I sat to exchange my slippers for jogging shoes.

"No. That's why I put up the dog gate. Letting him on the throw rug is like letting a camel put his nose in the tent during the desert nomad's time. Pretty soon he would take over and wreck the tent."

"Do you have to be so dogmatic?" I frowned. Seconds passed as I reflected, *Steve is being practical— I'm always the lenient one, even sneaking Benji treats from our table.*

In this case, I don't want to replace our carpet again, so I need to accept the barrier as necessary. Benji still has a nice bed right outside the bedroom door and we leave the door open so he can see us. Since I want something one way, I can't have it another—both ways.

The truth is—the gate exists because Benji, my little shadow, will try to get closer to me if he is in the room...my shadow. He wants to be right where I am. We have to limit him with outside barriers, because he refuses to obey. He has no motivation other than his driving obsession to be near me.

When God gives us rules and we dislike them, it is like Steve setting boundaries to limit where Benji can roam in the house.

Sometimes, I am not happy with Steve's discipline, but I admire his consistency.

Benji's new limitation gives him access to us—just not all the time. But really, we don't even have access to each other all the time. God is the only one who gets that privilege. And I'm not God—even Benji's.

My comfort in my suffering is this; Your promises preserve my life. ~Psalm 119:50

Lord, help me accept the limits you have given us to live in peace with Benji during this stage of his life and to realize he will adjust, and I will too.

Rescue

My friend, Tom, took in a stray rescue Shepherd, so fearful, he tucked himself under Tom's trailer home for a week. Skye slid out shaking, eyes downcast, just long enough to grab an uneasy bite and retreat—backing into watch position. Over time Tom was able to feed Skye in the open, his front legs braced for another quick retreat.

Each time Skye ate, he lingered a little longer. This eventually rolled into weeks where he finally became a pet and guard dog for Tom's tree business. It took time for his natural bent to be a protector, as Shepherds are, to emerge. First, he had to be nourished and healed of his fear of humans and become a kept dog. Once cared for and accepting of his keeper, he could fulfill his purpose in being what God meant him to be.

A year later, I watched Skye for a week during Tom's vacation. Skye accepted pats and walked eagerly with me and my dog, Mickey, confident to explore the fields surrounding us, even chasing the pitched balls. He was a changed animal—a pet.

When we use the word "rescue," what comes to mind? Mainly, we think of animals with abusive owners.

The dog has lived somewhere between hard times and horrible times. It could be horrible because masters physically abused the dog with a threatening voice, a mean glare…an overpowering hand. The dog cringes…or hides. We can't see the wounds. They are invisible, but given the right circumstances or similar situations, the psyche inside emits an "ouch," a howl. Or, the animal was severely neglected. No kind touch, no care. Nothing.

One is not worse than the other, necessarily. Either produces a mental, emotional, and physical wreck. Both situations can be reversed and directed toward health given the time and attention required…sometimes daunting. It can take years, even their lifetime.

Commitment to nurture an animal or a relationship takes dogged determination. It's obviously easier to train a new pup than take in an old dog with old ways, or wounds. It is a given—we never know in the beginning what lies ahead.

As a newlywed, I reeled from the exasperated voice of my husband, disappointed by my failure to respond the way he hoped. For example, the attention I neglected to give him when he came home—like he did me. He often greeted me in the garage as I pulled the car in. It never dawned on me to drop whatever I was doing, rather than finish, and rise eagerly to greet him like our dog did—like I'm really glad to see him. He thought I would just *know*. And he didn't get I need words expressed on cards, especially for holidays and special occasions. As a writer, I thought he'd just *know*. We'd howl at each other.

False expectations lead to resentments. However,

sometimes resentments are built upon past experiences too. More of the same and similar actions from partners that did not lead to feeling secure in a relationship snowball into the present. We may misread and mistake each other's intentions as from another person, someone who hurt us deeply. Or we may take things personally, when it has nothing to do with us. Our spouse may forget to check their text messages, prefer to ride their bike alone at times, and really not notice they spent too much on groceries—again. That is their nature. We can't make a schnauzer a Lab.

Our hearts can grow cold if change seems too slow…we lose hope. *When is he, she, the dog…going to change? They are, this is…so much work!* Anger can emerge, and words that pierce like a sword—hurtful words. Acceptance stands at the door, knocking at our hearts, for peace.

Whether married or single, by the time many of us mature as adults, we have been injured from past relationships. We marry and the experiences, ours and theirs, are carried into this new relationship. No wonder the Honeymoon Phase can quickly shift into the next developmental stage of marriage—the Disappointment Phase.

We are not who they hoped we'd be…or we hoped we'd be. They are not that amazing person who is reasonably patient and compassionate with all our gaps. And maybe, we get easily aggravated, annoyed at their gaps. You know—the things they "should" have learned by this season of their lives. As the gaps grow larger, the grace grows smaller... *if we focus* on the gaps.

How did you stay married for 30 years? I have asked many a friend. Or 20? Or 40?

All my life I have heard a one word answer emphasized. "GOD!"

My husband and I are at nine years and we have come to the same conclusion.

How do we stay committed to someone we've pledged to nurture when the quirks pass from months into years?

The Acceptance phase. You've heard it, "God grant me the wisdom to accept the things I cannot change, courage to change the things I can... and wisdom to know the difference."

God alone gives us patience to wait for better times—when we can discover the purpose we bring to each other. In part, it is to protect each other—to be each other's keeper. To be each other's rescuer.

Devastation may have come through others, but we will trust in the Lord until the season of disaster has passed and the air is calm again. We can move toward health of mind, body and soul. If we aggravate old wounds by our own ignorance—rash words, actions, and impulsive decisions—we can receive forgiveness and learn better ways of coping. By asking God for patience and perseverance, we can all learn new behaviors and change together.

We need His help to live side-by-side in day-to-day life, until the scale feels more balanced—feeling less frustration from just maintaining—to feeling more pleasure from companionship. The shift happens.

Slowly, man or beast know what to expect around us and alter some behaviors. We can accept their quirks that triggered us to chase our own tails. The eyes of acceptance enlarge and embrace the dog, the spouse, and our daily companions, quicker. In time, their love and loyal devotion imprints a deep joy in our hearts. Their sour side or crazy quirks, patterns and idiosyncrasies, spark our silly bone—and a knowing grin.

Eventually, we realize we have been learning as much from them as they have been learning from us. We are shifting our behaviors as much as they are. They are accepting and reworking our judgments as much as we are being affected and evaluating theirs.

Over time, similarities in spouses appear as much as dogs and masters tend to look the same...like they really are related. The truth is, maybe God rescued us, each and all, man and beast—and He put us together for a bigger picture.

Maybe His plan was to give us to each other, two-legged and four-legged companions, to share life and family and love.

But when the kindness and love of God our Savior appeared, he saved us, not because of righteous things we had done, but because of his mercy. ~ Titus 3:4

Lord, thank You for Your love that rescues us from wounds that cause selfishness, or independence. For giving us fresh perspectives and greater understanding through those You've brought into our lives to live beside us on a daily basis. You placed us together for a purpose. Today, remind us to offer ourselves grace for our shortcomings and offer those around us affirmations and positive strokes, so we all feel valued and valuable, as Your creation.

Thank You for these precious ones, these big and little companions, human and furry, beloved friends and family—who are different than us. Because of them we are more understanding and compassionate people. Because of You, we're empowered to grow a deeper bond of commitment—our higher calling to love that perseveres, that hopes all things, endures all things— that suffers long and is kind. It is only because of You, we know unconditional love. It is only through You, we can freely give . . . as we've been given.

The following section includes five devotionals
about the time our pets leave us…

There is a time for everything and a
season for every activity under heaven.
A time to be born and a time to die.
~Psalm 23:4

Just like us, our doggies get sick, have accidents, age.
There comes a time when we carry them
to the Rainbow Bridge. It is a hard walk.
But we stay close to them, as they always have to us.

These devotions are meant to strengthen you
To help you through this passage…
To grant you the peace that you are
a comfort to your fur babies to the end.
To give hope to all of us longing to hug our pets again.
Someday soon…in doggie heaven.

Shelby's Crossover

When Mickey, my first mini schnauzer, was old and sick, my thoughts rummaged and circled back to his condition, even at work. Every day I tried to decipher what to do next in caring for my aged canine. One early pre-op shift, I spoke with a patient about Mickey's absent stares and how he ran into corners and stood there—unable to back up. I would literally have to pick him up and turn him around. He was fourteen.

That morning God gave me a very special exchange through the heart of my patient.

"My Dalmatian was thirteen years old; she was tired." The woman lying on the gurney in her hospital gown seemed completely comfortable and calm as she began to share her dog story while awaiting surgery.

"I still remember how she would just sit and watch me in the kitchen." Her faint smile retraced a pleasant memory. "One day I stopped, and we just stared at each other. Neither of us flinched. It was very spiritual." She continued speaking softly. "Our eyes connected. We just looked at each other in silence one last time, just as we had done so many times through the years." I could feel her pain of letting go.

"It was one of those moments when you know

you both know what you're thinking. 'Okay, Shelby,' I nodded at my beautiful old girl. 'It's okay if you cross over.'"

That's all I said. She understood.

I drove to the store a little while later to get some groceries. I was gone no longer than an hour. When I walked back into the kitchen, she was gone." She paused…then continued.

"I felt like Shelby was hanging on for me. I had to let go when I was ready. She just needed me to say it." I felt my eyes moisten as she described a little more about her special girl.

"When I got her, she was skittish and thin—a rescue dog, she'd been beaten and starved. She was at the vet for two months before she was ready to adopt. I picked her up, and then left her home for a brief while to do some shopping. When I drove back up the driveway an hour later, I looked and looked again. My husband was playing with her. They had bonded instantly."

"In later years she had heart problems. The first time we took her in for the symptoms the gruff old vet spent three hours with her! He was the best vet. He put her on heart pills. Then at the second visit, she went to find him in the back room! He was *her* vet. He was wonderful. I spent almost ten grand on her medical problems."

"Wow!" I felt amazed at her investment.

"I'd do it again." She smiled.

After that day, I began to pray with my little Mickey every night about Doggie Heaven.

After that day, I felt like I could let go if Mickey needed me to.

God used that day and Shelby's story to prepare me for Mickey's story.

Many waters cannot quench love; rivers cannot wash it away. If one were to give all of the wealth of his house for love, it would be utterly scorned.

~ Song of Solomon 8:7

Dear Lord, thank You for the amazing spiritual connection we feel with our animals. Thank You for their simple ways, their simple faith in us, in life and in their own way…in You.

Help us to trust Your timing and Your knowledge of these beautiful creatures You destined when it is their time to crossover to Doggie Heaven. We entrust them back to You, just as You entrusted them to man a long time ago in Paradise.

It's Friday but Sunday's Coming

One Friday afternoon, groceries shifted in the back seat as I made a sharp-right into home base and up my driveway.

The garage door rose slowly, as Pepper, my two-year-old miniature schnauzer, flew out. I opened my car door to pat his head…and missed. His head bent and lowered, his eyes shifted across the street and suddenly—he sprang. I called out and turned just in time to see him dribbled between the bottom of a large white truck and the pavement in front of my house. Seconds later, I knelt over his limp body no more than ten feet from the mailbox.

Sammy stood on the sidewalk, eyes wide and tail wagging wild. The street was strangely quiet except for the sound of my own voice screaming, "Oh my God. My baby!"

I watched a scene that would replay over and over again in my head the next 48 hours. My mind filmed the graphic details of Pepper underneath the truck—a horror footage I could not splice from my memory.

Sunday at church, I stood next to my dear friend, Karen, a cat lady. Tears welled up again—my voice cracked during worship. "I can't get the scene of

Pepper's death out of my mind." I grieved, feeling broken and tormented by the haunting clip.

"Take it to God," she patted my shoulder. "He knows your grief."

"But I keep seeing Pepper underneath the truck and his screams afterward. I can't stand it!" I said breaking down again.

"But he is not feeling that anymore." Karen stroked my shoulder trying to comfort me. "He is in heaven with Mickey, they are together. Imagine him there now."

"Yes, I bet they are sliding down rainbows and hopping on the clouds." I smiled wearily. Picturing the two of them together, the silver and the black, in a beautiful garden of lush trees at peace in Paradise and the presence of God and His angels lifted my spirits.

"Let's pray," she said. We joined hands and Karen prayed that I would know Pepper is okay now and he is happy in doggie heaven. *He knows I love him and one day we will all be together again.* "Help Dee see Pepper and his little personality the way she knew him and the way he is now. Please take away the memory of that brief time of his physical death that is over now."

I listened to her prayer doubting it would make a difference. I had been trying not to think about it the past 48 hours. But by the time the service ended something strange happened. I kept seeing him and Mickey frolicking together in their heavenly home. I smiled at the thought.

My heavy heart lightened in the light of my faith

and trust in the gentle Shepherd who created and loves sheep, not only the human ones.

Exactly a week later on Sunday morning, I led singing at Juvenile Hall. Looking out at some of the downtrodden faces, I remembered how God intervened in my life so miraculously and comforted my hurting heart in a way I never thought possible this time last week.

Now, I wondered what some of these boys had been through. Would it help them to hear the story of Pepper's death and how God helped me work through the trauma of that experience? Had they ever seen something they wished they hadn't? Had anyone ever prayed with them about their haunting? *Where do we put our mortal grief if we have no heavenly hope?*

"I would like to share something that happened to me last week when I lost my two-year-old schnauzer," I began sharing my experience, thoughts and feelings from Friday afternoon to Sunday morning—and encouraged them to pray and take their scene to heaven's gates.

My brother began teaching. I decided to head out early. Just before the door closed behind me, a female guard caught it and stood to talk to me in the hallway, jamming her foot in the door to prop it open.

"I just want to tell you something," she whispered. "Right after you shared, a young boy in the back called me over. He said he 'saw his brother killed and he cannot stop thinking about it.' He wants your brother to pray with him after the service today."

"Thank you for sharing that with me." My heart welled up in marvel of God's timing.

Somehow God turned everything wrong that happened into something good, something that could help this young boy find his way out of his hole. I felt better *knowing* he would find solace turning to God for comfort just as I had.

"Thank You, Lord," I whispered, "for turning something good out of even this, only the way You can."

And we know that all things work together for good to them that love God, to them who are the called according to his purpose. ~ Romans 8:28 (KJV)

Thank You, Lord. You bring light to our darkness and heaven's hope to our mortal grief. You are the good Shepherd. Thank You for walking with us through the valley of the shadow of death, and for the reality of Paradise where we will be safe with You forever.

Divine Interruptions

Mickey thumped against the back of my seat as I jammed on the brakes, narrowly missing the car ahead. It had pulled out of the parking lot past the first empty lane—directly in front of me. Although in a rush to make a Saturday night dinner party, I glared at the ladies engrossed in conversation through the back window of their luxury car and turned around to assess the damage to my whimpering dog. Mickey's eyes winced as he looked up at me, holding his front left paw at an odd almost 90 degree angle.

Disgusted and angry at the oblivious driver, I pulled my pet up onto my lap as he held his leg out, so convoluted, it seemed to be broken. He was still whimpering when we stopped by the house long enough to inform the dinner host of my sudden emergency and assess his little legs. He walk-skipped on three legs, until he lost his balance... and rolled to the side.

My stomach sank knowing the dinner I had been looking forward to was off. Now, I anticipated a hefty vet bill and a crippled dog. Bad timing—or was it?

Standing at the veterinary desk completing Mickey's visit I still stewed, the bill double what humans pay at their corner "doc in a box." The vet assessed no apparent break. I refused the x-ray to check for certain. "That's OK, I'll wait to see how he's faring tomorrow," I stated matter-of-factly.

As I turned around in time to see Mickey piddling on the floor, a man shoved through the entrance with such force he almost sent Mick flying. Mumbling "sorry," he grimly paced, squeezing a limp golden cocker spaniel tightly to his chest.

"I think he's dead," the woman behind him cried, wiping away tears. Then she looked at me and said, "I backed over him in the driveway."

"I'm so sorry..." I shuddered unable to imagine how hard that would be.

Compassion welled through me as I found myself stating, "accidents happen."

"But it's not even my dog," she groaned."We were watching him. He's fifteen years-old and deaf. He can't see well and..."

Empathy guided me. "My dog is fourteen and I consider every day I have him past thirteen a privilege. His Rottweiler friend died at eight years old which is not unusual for bigger breeds. If my dog were hit, I'd accept it. I'd rather he be hit and go quickly than drag on through the years or months struggling. Truly."

The lady looked up searching my eyes.

I used to work in the ER. Life is wonderful, but it's also hard—there are a lot of accidents. "I've been a nurse a long time and I've seen a lot of death—people of all ages in all situations, trauma and illness. I saw a five-year-old who was run over and died. But I believe that only God can allow a life to end. Sometimes he picks his flowers young, sometimes, older. I do believe he picks them though, people and animals too—all his creation."

The lady seemed to calm down. I walked over and patted her arm as she quietly wept.

Minutes later the vet assistant returned to the front desk to inform them the dog had passed on. Somehow I felt God wanted me to be here now to help these people process their tragedy. His timing is perfect, just as I'd told my nephew earlier that day before he left for school and I went about my errands— before Mickey's accident. We had read from Proverbs 16:9 together, "Man makes his plans but God directs his steps."

And somehow, now, it was all as it was supposed to be. I was meant to be here in the Dog ER tonight, mourning with these neighbors in my community—not at the dinner party laughing with my friends. By the time Mickey and I headed home, his leg sprained but not broken, I was content to settle into a quiet evening alone.

There is a time for everything, and a season for every activity under heaven: a time to be born and a time to die ... a time to weep and a time to laugh, a time to mourn and a time to dance ...

~ Ecclesiastes 3:1–2, 4

Lord, thank you for the interruptions and trials we so despise but that are meant to teach us patience and perspective. May we see more of your higher view in all the details that delay, and trials that distress us and test our patience. Have your way in us now so You can use even the most unpleasant situations for good as we release our will to Your ways at all times.

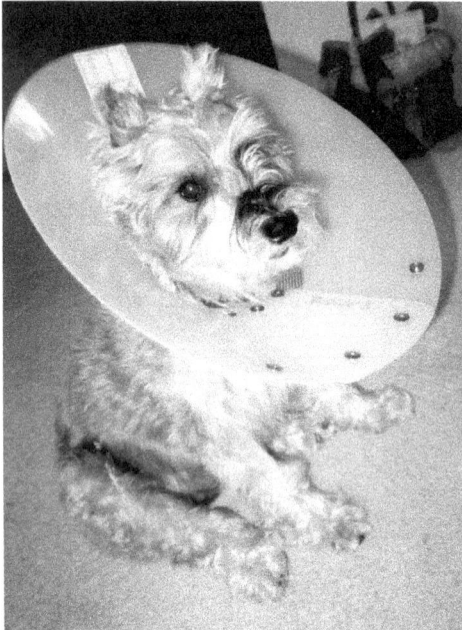

Happy Tails to You
Until We Meet Again

I woke up before 3:00 a.m. to the sound of weak cries coming from the garage.

"Steve, get up. It's Sam."

Throwing on my robe—I knew. I ran to the kitchen, grabbed some pain pills and crushed them to make a paste Sam would possibly swallow through his syringe.

We had arrived home the day before from Tahoe. Benji ran to meet us the moment the garage door lifted. His head darted around, looking everywhere—at Steve, across the street—but not at me. *Unusual behavior.* He shifted his body and whimpered. I scooped him up and rocked him.

"Where's Sam?" Steve looked around and answered in the same breath, "Gary must have taken him out."

Puzzled, I looked around. *No sign of Gary's truck. He would have taken him earlier before he left from dog-sitting.*

I put Benji down, who was still unable to make eye

contact. We followed him around to the backyard. He stepped into the ivy and backed up abruptly, staring from the patio into the green. *Odd.* We traced his gaze into the shady corner of the yard. Sam peered at us through the green foliage, only his big yellow head visible.

Steve brushed past me. "I can't coax him up. His legs are shaking."

Inside the house we discovered a large puddle of bile on the living room floor.

"We don't know how long, Steve. It may be a day it may be a week." I was numb. We had been in and out of the vet many times the past six months—and spent way too much on vet bills.

I called Gary.

"Sammy was fine. He played with the ball, drank a lot of water and ate heartily. He was full of life." Gary hesitated. "I hope you don't mind. I let him sleep with me in the guest room. I thought this may be the last time we can do that."

When I walked into the garage, Sam was standing by the door. "Steve, Sam's here." I stroked Sam's soft head. Breathing heavy, his heart and his eyes looked dull as he stared straight ahead. "This may be it, Steve. His eyes are not focused and they seem to go out to the side." We guided him to his garage bed and said good night.

Syringe in hand, I approached Sam. He lay on the garage floor ten feet from his dog bed, between the car and washer. I administered the dose between his teeth.

He grunted weakly, his body stiff as his tail, and the medicine ran out. His glassy eyes stared straight ahead. Listless, his tongue lay in folds like a curtain flowing over his canines onto the cement.

That mouth, that tail—my Lab. I remembered the first time I saw him. The owner handed me one of two yellow males. I cuddled the first, stared in his little face, and then looked up. The breeder held out Sam, ready to hand him to me next. *What a sweet face.* Our eyes locked—it was instant. I passed the brother back, embraced Sammy, and held on to him—forever smitten.

American Greeting Cards accepted Sammy's puppy photo three months later for their calendar. I snapped him sitting on the back of a cross-country ski as he peered up at me. He paused in-between somersaults, flipping himself off the wood and tumbling into the snow he loved. That photograph became my first publication. Sam had been my good luck charm from the very beginning.

"Sammy loves singing, Steve. He always comes to join me when I play guitar." I sang, bending over Sam and stroked his head and back.

Steve joined me.

"'What a fellowship, what a joy divine, leaning on the everlasting arms...'" I started.

Steve followed with "Jesus loves me this I know" and explained, "I always sang that to my boys growing up."

Normally, a living heater, Sam's legs and paws felt cool to touch. *The time is getting closer.*

"It's okay, Sammy. Go be with Jesus and Mickey and Pepper. You've been a good dog. I love you, Sammy. One day we will see each other again when we all come back together again in our heavenly home."

Sam's breathing grew soft and shallow, his mouth opened and closed like alligator jaws, slow and purposeful, as if he wanted to bark one last time but couldn't. Mucus dripped from my nose.

Lord, send doggie angels to take him home. Take his pain away. I looked over his precious gaunt face and waited, tracing a path from the bridge of his nose to his ears. How I would miss flipping his ears and curling them in my hands.

"You lived a good life and you are having a good death here with us."

Running my fingers over his paws, I thought back to the vet's office Easter Sunday two weeks prior.

"You might want to put him down, if he's in pain," the vet had said.

I gazed at Sam sitting squalid and still, breathing easily and looked back at the young vet in blue scrubs for the second time in three days. "No, Sam is peaceful. I don't mind if he dies at home."

Another vet looked at his x-rays with me again. "Can I show you them so you can make the right decision?"

I followed her down the hall. This was the second time here and I already resisted more tests than necessary this time. $1,500 in four months, we could not keep paying for Sam's treatments. If he was to live, he would kick this thing. He stopped eating and drinking for three days and began vomiting everything. As soon as he lapped water a few times a little puddle of green appeared. It seemed the cancer had come back after five years.

"These are nodules all over his lungs." She pointed to the x-ray on the wall. As you can see, he hardly has a sliver of a lung on the left." I stared at the black dots scattered over the larger white blurry area.

"Sam has had respiratory problems since he was a puppy." I could still remember hearing him snort and whistle from his puppy crate.

"And here's a mass. We don't know what it is without further work up, but the other vet agrees. It's all leading to cancer."

Tears filled her eyes. Mine were empty. The reservoir was down after the last few days. I felt peace, not panic, as I had the other two times we had rushed him here groaning and crying from the car to a stretcher.

Her face looked sad. "We really have no options if you don't want to go on with more tests so we can see what we can do."

I looked at the foreboding films and spoke. "Many patients I have had through the years have lived with cancer and terrible bodies. Sometimes the cancer is cured and reappears as it seems it may have in Sam. If they don't want to eat or drink, just like Sam, they stop. It's okay. They are at peace at home and on pain meds." I felt confident.

"If he stops drinking, we will keep him comfortable. If he is in pain we will bring him in. Sam is at peace. I'm happy to take him home and let him die if it is to be now."

"He had a good death." I sat on the garage floor surprised by my own calm, stroking Sam's still golden head and warm limp ear. Steve stood inches away from Sam's straight lifeless tail.

"Really, I don't know." His face ashen, he spoke of his dearly loved Slate, a black Lab/retriever who lived to fourteen. "The vet took Slate to the back before he died because he was having seizures. I wasn't with him."

I rested my hand on the familiar brow. "Sam was straining, but he calmed when we got here. He has been peaceful these last few minutes. It's just like that with people when I worked in the hospital. You want to pray with them, sing with them, just be with them in their passing. You don't want them to be alone." I stroked his cold paw.

"It is a privilege." Steve sniffed.

"My yellow Lab, Sam, just passed away. He's nine and a half," I called the UC Davis Vet Hospital Emergency room at 3:30 a.m. and explained. "Five years ago Sam was at UC Davis a lot—they thought he was going to die. They used him as a learning patient for their rounds and asked if I would donate his body for study when he died. He had a miracle turn-around and we've had him another five years. So, I'm calling to see if you still want his body for study. We've known he was on his way out these last couple weeks. I just wanted him to die at home. He had a peaceful passing."

The woman's voice sounded soft. "To me, it's kind of the ideal situation if they can die at home."

I felt gratitude. "Yeah, me too."

After we hung up, I turned to Steve standing near me in the office.

"My relief is that there wasn't a lot of pain and we were here." I sat in my chair holding Kleenex. Steve wiped away a tear from his face with his hand. Benji lie curled in his bed. Minutes after Sam died, Steve woke Benji up. Benji trotted straight through the house garage entrance past me and Sam's body a few feet away— straight to Sam's bed. He sniffed it, turned around and beelined into the house again. He only glanced briefly at me when Steve admonished him. He had already said his goodbye yesterday, we surmised.

"That's how it was with Mom," Steve reflected now. "I wasn't with her the weekend she died. I said goodbye on Wednesday. My sister and I knew it was her last week. We all visited and talked. She was really coherent the Sunday before. It was then she told me, 'It's okay, Steve, if you are not here when I die.'

"But on Wednesday I took a day off work and drove back to the Bay Area. That last time I saw her, we said our sincerest loving goodbyes. We didn't talk. We just held hands and told each other we loved each other. The last words we spoke I said, 'I love you.' And Mom looked at me and said, 'I love you, Steve.' Three days later, she passed and I wasn't there, but I was at peace."

I looked at my new husband, appreciative for his significant final moments with the mother-in-law I will never meet. *How we say goodbye to those we love, whether people or animals, is so important.*

"That's my relief," I looked at Steve. "I think I grieved three weeks ago when I cried for three days over Easter and all our family was here. It's just like with people. By the time it comes, sometimes the grieving has been done before."

I thought back seven months, weeks before our wedding. Two of those stressful weeks were spent nursing Sam. One of those nights I slept with a blanket by him on the floor weeping. "Sam, I can't be happy on my wedding day if you're not there. I need you to be there." Benji and Sam were to walk up the aisle with my wedding party. Sam and I locked eyes many times that long dark winter night. My tears flowed freely as I stroked him and searched his chocolate brown eyes, sad and knowing. I left him numerous times making calls between two emergency vets, agonizing over opinions and the course to take.

Steve spoke with tenderness. "Sammy hung on so we had more enjoyment. And I got the pleasure of living with him for five months."

In those five months living day in and day out with Sam, Steve taught him "gentle," to lift food from our hands rather than bite our fingers off. He trained him to wait on the "rug" while we ate instead of drooling by the table. In those months, Steve grew to love Sam. He loved him so he could grieve him. Sam knew that would be important to me. It was his final gift.

Yet what we suffer now is nothing compared to the glory he will give us later. For all creation is waiting patiently and hopefully for that future day when God will resurrect his children. For on that day thorns and thistles, sin, death, and decay—the things that overcame the world against its will at God's command—will all disappear, and the world around us will share in the glorious freedom from sin which God's children enjoy. For we know even the things of nature, like animals and plants, suffer in sickness and death as they await this great event. ~ Romans 8:18–22 (TLB)

Lord, thank You for showering me with life and love through the life of Sam. Thank You for the loving creature You created, a heavenly companion who guarded me during a time of much physical weakness and dark mental tunnels the past decade. You knew what was to come then. You knew I would need his strength and protection to feel safe, his faithfulness and loyalty to feel accepted, his warmth and joy to feel hope and happiness.

He brought the presence and peace You give straight from Paradise to help me persevere and find the yellow brick road again, to reach this new brighter chapter I've only just begun.

Sam will always be our family dog. His gifts and greeting were unlike none other. He blessed each of us with his joy and positive energy over and over again.

Thank You, Father, for the celebration of Sam and his life well lived. What we shared together brought far more than words could ever express. Keep him safe and happy in Doggie Heaven with all the doggie angels…until we meet again.

> "Don't cry because it's over,
> Smile because it happened."
> ~ Dr. Seuss

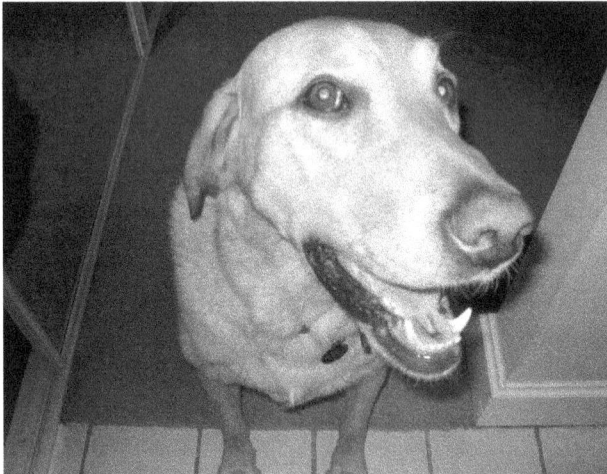

Doggie Heaven

"Benji, soon you are going to be in heaven. No more scary nights." I looked into the dazed eyes of my little schnauzer with doggie dementia, sitting in front of the refrigerator. He groaned.

I stroked his head and held out a treat...our second round tonight. It was 2am.

"He's resisting the medicine," my husband, Steve, remarked every evening as Benji fought laying in his bed despite various medications. It seemed he was afraid—his fears magnified in the dark. He was deaf and cataracts dulled his once shining eyes.

I'd been praying, hoping Benji would die in his sleep. Steve and I had passed the one year mark taking turns with him multiple times a night. First the sound of paws, then whining at our door until one of us offered to "get up this time."

Finally, it was time—time for us to help Benji cross Rainbow Bridge. I had called and cancelled two vet appointments. I couldn't cancel again...I pushed myself a little harder. "God, help me," led the prayers the day we completed Benji's final lap in the neighborhood he'd walked for fourteen years...

Bring his bed. A thought surfaced. "Thank you, Lord. Good idea." I felt a little better.

When we arrived at the vet, Steve stayed in the waiting room and I carried Benji and his bed into the exam room. His shaking stopped instantly when I placed him on the soft familiar fur.

The techs came and went from the room. Benji cooperated with the quick exam, strangely still—head turned with his eyes fixed on mine the whole time.

"Sammy's waiting to greet you, Benji," I stroked his enchanting soft ears, cherishing the moment. Our eyes lingered. "Jesus will be with you in heaven and Mommy will see you again when I get there…"

Benji's muscles felt relaxed—he was truly calm.

The vet hooked the syringe into Benji's leg IV catheter. In less than ten seconds Benji's head slumped. He sank into his bed as though asleep.

When I met Steve in the waiting room I explained, "My last look at Benji was as if he was conked out in his bed after a walk…but this time he fell asleep on earth and he'll wake up in doggie heaven."

Later, at home, I read Psalms twenty-three. Now, verse four meant so much more to me… "Even though I walk through the valley of the shadow of death I will fear no evil, for you are with me."

I had asked God to help me walk through this day and had dreaded it. I had avoided it for months. I even felt sick about it…hoping for an easier way…that Benji die naturally.

But, Benji was okay—his final day. He felt secure as long as I was near him. He did not fear evil or death in his bed, his safe place, with me standing next to him. Benji was at peace.

He was at peace with me as much as I felt peace walking through death's door with my little guy, my little shadow ... because God was with me.

Even though I walk through the valley of the shadow of death, I will fear no evil, For you are with me ...

~ Psalm 23:4

Thank You, Lord, for being our Good Shepherd, and walking through the valley of death with us as we part with our most precious doggies. We are grateful for the strength and stamina You give us, to be a loving presence that brings them peace to the end, knowing one fine day Your loving presence will comfort us on our last terrestrial lap.

Circle of Life

"Look at Lily on the dishwasher," Steve hollered from the family room. I turned from the sink where I stood rinsing the breakfast plates and looked down at Lily, our twelve-week-old Australian Labradoodle. Her chocolate nose twitched, aimed toward the dirty dishes inside as she perched on the open door. "I haven't seen that since Sam." Steve laughed.

My mind rewound to one of my favorite memories of Sam at three months. "I have a picture of Sam in that same position... in fact the same dishwasher—from fifteen years ago," I told Steve.

How many pictures of Sam and Benji are stored in the iCloud? Probably more in boxes, as then I still used disposable cameras and had prints made. Times change. But no need to dig up the photo—I could still see that delightful moment of Sammy lasered in my cortex. Lifetimes of pictures stored in places years can't erase—precious memories—the Sam and Benji years.

Not a week goes by and we don't think of Sam and Benji. Last year when Benji passed, I promised my husband I'd wait two years before getting another dog. He wanted to do road trips in our retirement without encumbrance.

But November, six months after Benji joined Sam in doggie heaven, sadness gripped me in a strange way.

"You need a dog." My ninety-five-year-old Dad stated randomly one day at his assisted living. The following week as he headed into the house from our garage, heavy on his walker, he looked down passing the spot Sam's plate used to be. "Yep, you need a dog."

"I told Steve I'd wait a couple years until we could travel." I meant what I promised. But I never promised I'd be happy about it.

The tears started in November...when I'd see people walking their dogs. Hugging their dogs.

It began to remind me of my early thirties when I'd cry seeing children at church or in strollers on a jog...or talking in groups with friends and their babies. That wasn't God's plan for me. Now that so many mid-lifers were becoming grandparents, I'd noticed a familiar sadness brush my emotions as I scrolled Facebook posts and announcements—a hint of past pain. Somehow, God was preparing to comfort me once again.

"Honey," Steve stared at my distraught expression one morning as we neared Thanksgiving. "I want a dog. You need a dog."

We discussed it and agreed on two. Dogs are pack animals. I soon discovered no other schnauzer would replace Benji. *I can't do that to another dog*; *I just need a different breed*. But what breeds? Steve needed hypoallergenic and no shedding. We both had back issues. They would need to be around twenty pounds. It was Covid year—the rescues and shelters were empty.

I'd seen many Australian shepherds when I hiked. Upon inquiry, the owners would reply with enthusiasm "great! We love our dogs" and "yes, they do shed a lot."

Steve and I had both owned Lab mixes before we met. We loved their happy temperaments. I had just learned of Australian Labradoodles, a small Lab doodle with a cocker spaniel twist bred originally to be companion, service dogs. Bingo.

So the internet search began for aussiedoodles and Australian Labradoodles. I filled out applications and joined breeders' waiting lists from coast to coast.

Steve and I prayed one day in the family room. "Lord, we don't know what we're doing, but please pick which of these breeds would be best to raise first and we'll trust you for when we add the second pup." We had no idea at the time just how much we would need to trust God for so much more.

Thanksgiving week a breeder from Texas I'd spoken to on Friday, emailed on Sunday morning. "Matilda's whelping. The litter is picked in order of when I receive your deposit." I wanted a blue merle male so we venmoed our money immediately. Steve wanted to name the first puppy, so he decided on Lassen—the name of his favorite national park.

Mid-December we had third choice when the breeder called on pick day. The male was taken, so our Lassen became a beautiful female blue merle, the calmest—the runt—of the litter. My friend Nancy also picked one of Lassen's lively litter mates, Quigley, for her children's Christmas gift.

Late January I flew to Dallas to pick up Lassen. But not before Steve's occupational therapist had warned Steve, "You two can't get a puppy. You're both in chaos." She had just fitted Steve with a sock putter-oner-thingy, so he could put his own sock on following surgery. And I was still hopping on crutches.

In one week, timid Lassen transformed into a bundle of energy, complete with light-speed zoomies and alligator puppy bites. Our arms looked like teething boards. She loved tug of war, fetching balls, pulling our clothes, and chewing endless toys we bought to distract her from biting, biting, and more biting. We had our hands full.

Besides this, Lassen had three stubborn parasites and unending treatments that would keep her from doggie training and other dogs for months. Never take a puppy to a dog-friendly hotel—I learned the hard way. I wish I'd taken a turn-around flight and not exposed Lassen to whatever bugs strange dogs carried into the hotel room.

By the time July rolled around we had passed on three litters from the Australian Labradoodle breeder although we had put a deposit down in December Covid year. We were eightieth on the waiting list at that time.

"I can't be Lassen's playmate anymore, Steve. She needs another dog." I would moan as we passed up another Labradoodle litter, not yet ready for puppy number two.

"But I'm not well enough to help train or clean up yet." Steve felt bad.

Exhausted, I couldn't fill the play-dog role she needed. "Wow, Dee, I've never seen a dog with so much energy," friends remarked. We called her "bullet" when she zoomed in the morning and at night.

I felt deep down in my knower, Lassen needed another dog and we would be okay. So in spite of Steve's not feeling quite ready, and friends warnings of "it's more work with two," we watched a video of litter-ready Australian Labradoodles on the breeder's website.

Even though I hoped for the little male, at the sight of one particular pup, Steve settled against the back of the couch and emitted a sigh. "That little female is sure mellow. It would be great to have a calm puppy." I had to agree as I watched the busy male bite and clawed the AstroTurf.

So we ended up with two female pups. Lily at eight weeks and Lassen at eight months. It was a match made in doggie heaven… after the first two weeks.

Initially, Lassen wasn't too keen on this little stranger drawing our affection, and we kept them apart. Soon, they were playing amidst our observation as we'd intervene to separate them when the yelps or growls began. Lassen herding Lily and never giving her a break. We set up a crate and gated area so Lily and Lassen could just peer and nose each other between times together. Our backyard fit the need for Lily's flurries and Lassen's need for zoomies and to leap on the raised perimeter as an obstacle course.

Lily still wakes at night crying after accidents.

Lassen paws the bell on the sliding back door to go out and uses her pee pads at night. Lassen rips up paper in a hot minute and shadows me like Benji. Not a lap dog, she squirms after being held too long. Lily is affectionate and tucks herself under Steve's legs on the couch where he spends a lot of time healing. She has amazing eye contact like Sam, like a Lab.

Lassen is the guard dog who hears and sees all. She is hypervigilant, and can go all day without sleeping. Lily likes her naps.

This morning I heard Steve say, utterly astonished, "Big gulps! Lick, lick. Chew, chew. Chop, chop."

Lily had run straight to Lassen's food bowl after inhaling her own breakfast. I forgot to pick it up. Lassen is a grazer and never eats much. We have to pick up her bowl and keep it away from Lily, like we once kept Benji's meals away from Sam. Truly Lily is a foodie. She typically has something dangling from her mouth, string, leaf, bark, etc. Lassen loves to chase balls, like Sam. Her circus-like agility and clown antics tickle our funny bones.

There are overlaps and twists of both Lassen and Lily. They are their own breeds. They are their own little personalities and characters. They have made Steve laugh like nothing else, now through his tenth month of rehab, following three surgeries, and waiting to drive again. Who would have known back when my spirit sagged with longing in November—there was a reason.

Before we got Lily, Steve felt apprehensive. He

reared and whinnied. "We can hardly do Lassen."

Lassen became so crazy excited when she saw other dogs because we had to wait so long to socialize her. The PetSmart trainer doubted she'd be calm enough to do group classes, that she'd missed her window of opportunity for socialization with other dogs.

Sure enough Lily helped. By the second week, both Steve and I noticed Lassen to be more calm… settled. She licks Lily's face and cleans it every morning. I guess just like humans need each other, dogs need other dogs to play with and frolic and help them to focus.

We know by our Lassen girl, who is sure shining lately, we made the right decision. Lily is a second blessing. God gave her to us at just the right time, just the right dogs—even the best order and picks of each litter—for an unduly hard season.

They are our furry comforts and bundles of joy. Lassen has her stuffed, comfort llama and pink pig and Lily has her teddy bears. We have them. They keep us busy early morning to night. I've never mopped the wood floors so much. But, we are retired… well semi. They are our girls and have brought laughter and fullness back into our home.

There have been a lot of difficult changes since Covid Christmas time, but here we are in winter with two new dogs we couldn't imagine life without, two smiles and two burgeoning hearts—no four.

And I think every time we talk about Sammy and Benji in regards to Lassen and Lily, they are both up there winking at each other. I can only imagine the four bursting hearts brimming with stories when Sammy

and Benji meet Lassen and Lily.
Such is the circle of life.

He has made everything beautiful in its time. He has also set eternity in the human heart; yet no one can fathom what God has done from beginning to end.
~ Ecclesiastes 3:11

Thank you, Lord, that especially when we feel confused and confined, unable to envision a future or plan, we can trust You see all that's to come. The darkness and light are both the same to you. Make it our instinct to trust You to be our guide, to protect us, and help us—one step, one dog, at a time.

Closing – Dog Family

We are dog lovers.

We have an uncanny need for dogs—dogs complete our family.

Our companions at work or play, they are at ease in our presence and we in theirs.

They help stabilize us as the storms of life rise and fall. They are predictable.

We feel positive around them. Playful. Even trusting, like children.

In a world of exhausting communication and misunderstandings, we bond with few words. They engage our emotions without the need for walls, and inspire childlike curiosity and adventure.

They evoke our nurturing side, demanding care and attention. They affect our attitude.

Sharing space—our lives, our homes, our yards with them—creates challenges that teach us how to compromise. We accommodate them and plan for them to live together in harmony. They bring us a daily song of joy from their morning greeting, to frequent check-ins, and goodnight paw-offerings.

They like our touch and crave our attention. We enjoy their nuzzles and loving gazes.

Our dogs have the capacity to make friends easily. They appreciate the smallest gestures of friendship with those they trust. It's not hard to understand why God placed them in Paradise to populate and procreate.

I believe God created dogs purposefully so we would live happier, feel safer, and experience love—an unconditional love that comes from God. They are His gift to us.

🐾

So the Lord God formed from the soil every kind of animal and bird, and brought them to the man to see what he would call them; and whatever he called them that was their name. ~ Genesis 2:19

About the Author

A retired hospital RN, Dee served in singles ministry and the Juvenile Justice Chaplaincy for over twenty-five years. Jesus Christ is the Light of her world—Dee's family and friends are her highlights.

Dee jokes she found her "heart of gold, Steve, as I was getting old" and married him in her nifty-fifties.

Granddaughter to immigrants, Dee loves cultural food and has traveled extensively, including missionary work. Both parents are lucid and feisty in their mid-nineties. The middle child between two brothers, she loves being an Aunt to her nephews.

Besides writing, poetry, and playing guitar, Dee and her husband enjoy nature hikes and bicycling together. Dee is a certified AFAA Piloga instructor.

Visit Dee at http://DeeAspin.com

Also by Dee Aspin

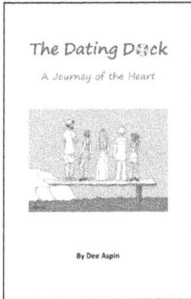

The Dating Dock: *A Journey of the Heart* (2018) Confused by dating? Is the person you are with marriage potential? Based on a dating metaphor, clarity is unpacked through poignant stories, Scriptures, winsome illustrations, and deep questions. This book relieves confusion Christians encounter as they navigate the stages of relationships.

Lord of the Ringless: *Devoted to God, Desiring Marriage* (2010) Decades of singleness and Single's Ministry inspired Dee's devotional Bible study, to equip and empower single Christians to pursue Christ as they seek to marry and fulfill their calling.

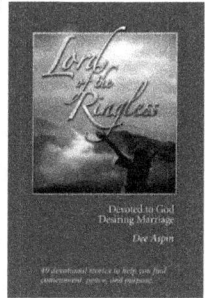

The ensuing faith-based stories narrated by a K-Love radio host, facilitated an introduction to Dee's husband, who earlier produced the inspirational audiobook, nominated for an Audie award.

dogSpirations (2015) Dee's principal characters, big and little canines, are Sammy and Benji featured in her own daily animal devotion. She revised and re-titled it, **Big and Little DogSpirations:** *We Love Them—They Inspire Us*. Available in ebook and audiobook.

Dee has written devotions for Upper Room, CBN, multiple animal compilations for Barbour Books and human-interest stories for Guideposts, Focus on the Family, Bethany House, Revel and more.

Visit Dee at: DeeAspin.com
Author Page: amazon.com/author/deeaspin.com

Dee's Stories also appear in:

Heavenly Humor for the Dog Lover's Soul: 75 Drool-Filled Inspirational Readings from Fellow Dog Devotees

Heavenly Humor for the Cat Lover's Soul: 75 Fur-Filled Inspirational Readings

The Dog Next Door and Other Stories of the Dogs We Love

Heaven Sightings: Angels, Miracles, and Glimpses of the Afterlife

3-Minute Devotions for a Dog Lover's Heart: 180 Paws-itively Perfect Readings

3-Minute Devotions for a Cat Lover's Heart: 180 Purr-fect Readings

True Stories of Extraordinary Answers to Prayer from Tragedy to Triumph

Inspired Glimpses of God's Presence, poetry

And, The Inspire Anthology Collection: Inspire Faith, Inspire Forgiveness, Inspire Joy, Inspire Love, and Inspire Promise,

www.ingramcontent.com/pod-product-compliance
Lightning Source LLC
Chambersburg PA
CBHW020848090426
42736CB00008B/288